Indian
Basket
Weaving

Indian Basket Weaving

How to Weave Pomo, Yurok,
Pima and Navajo Baskets

BY SANDRA CORRIE NEWMAN

 Northland Press

To the weavers:

Hilda Manuel, Mollie Jackson,

Rea Barber, Madeline Lewis,

Marie Lehi and her daughters

Contents

Foreword

RECURRENT REVIVALS OF INTEREST IN CRAFTS over the past hundred years, and the one now in progress, are evidence that we too, in the midst of abundance, can sense a form of cultural deprivation resulting from the supplanting of handicrafts by the cheap products of mechanized industry. For all but a few of us nowadays a large part of our life experience is swallowed up in the performance of small functions in giant operations of production, whereas in former days craft work was a creative, useful enterprise, an expression of individual ability and initiative that fitted harmoniously with the pioneer way of life. Little wonder that we look with nostalgic longing at the crafts of our ancestors and of the Indians.

Sandra Corrie Newman's offering is not meant to be a scientific report, although it contains aspects of Indian basketmaking not heretofore described. Rather, it unfolds for us her personal discovery, through long learning sessions, of the byways of traditional basketmaking of four different Indian tribes. Besides explicit information on gathering and preparation of natural materials and weaving techniques, she brings out the meaning of the craft to the partakers of these traditions. In the process, she captures the spirit of a fleeting moment in time just when the old traditions were about extinct and suddenly there comes renewed interest in them by both Indians and whites. The Indians are motivated by a sense of alarm that their native culture is about to fade away with the passing of the older generations; the whites are searching about for overlooked values missing from their own culture.

A previous movement of craft interest took place in the early 1900's spurred on by magazine articles, books, and hobby clubs. Much attention was focused on macrame work and basketmaking, in connection with which Indian basketry was recognized, praised, and to some extent copied. Although this movement generated great enthusiasm, the earnest hobbyists met their limits when they found that an investment of time was needed to perfect the appropriate skills, and that their works did not have any *necessary* utility as in the old days, but gave only a passing illusion of pioneer thrift. Museums now possess the outcome of this episode in the form of macrame bags and inconsequential-looking raffia baskets. However, values were experienced by the makers, if only temporarily, which were not otherwise provided by the conventional culture of that time.

Besides nostalgia, there is today a rising awareness and interest in the works of other traditions of culture. This awareness derives from the discoveries of anthropologists whose literature and insights have now to some degree reached the consciousness of the general public. What anthropologists found was that all cultures are somewhat exclusive and limiting in the patterns of life they prescribe, and that other cultures have discovered and developed values overlooked by our own. Youth also often finds as a revelation, upon reaching the age of questioning conventions, that our culture, indeed all cultures, tend to narrow upon a limited set of customs, beliefs, and values and to inhibit alternative behaviors. A common reaction is to ignore the accustomed ways of one's elders and look outward, often to other lands, for meaningful alternative modes of life.

There can be little doubt that the idea of making a utensil, tool, or item of wear directly from natural materials, especially *weaving* something, stirs deeply felt potentialities and inclinations to creativity within the human psyche. Not only can this tendency be seen repeatedly coming to the surface even under the most unpropitious circumstances, but it is observable in persons exploring these arts with concentration and singlemindedness that some essential value is being experienced, almost as a spiritual vitamin. Much is yet to be learned about mankind by taking account of his spontaneous activities in pleasure-giving pursuits. We can begin by experiencing for ourselves these stirrings and reflecting upon what it is that impels us. This book will give you the opportunity to do just that.

LAWRENCE E. DAWSON
Senior Museum Anthropologist
The Robert H. Lowie Museum of Anthropology

Preface

THIS BOOK is written, not only for women and men who live on the land, but also for collectors and admirers of American Indian crafts, that they may further appreciate the Indian basket with an understanding of the complexities of weaving.

For you who will take the time, and actually weave a basket, you will find that you have created a thing totally new and beautiful from the trees and grasses and roots around you. City shops are not necessary. Several weeks or months of good work will be needed, as will seasonal journeys to gathering places and reservations.

And after this time may come the knowledge that Bob Jackson, the son of my Pomo teacher, spoke of: "One's culture and heritage cannot be taught to someone without that person trying to live the life. We don't get our food, roots, etc. just any place, we have certain places to get these things. Mostly for quantity, but all these places are now closed so our way of life is also closed."

It is my hope that this book will help to keep the old way of life somewhat open.

Acknowledgments

THIS STUDY was originally conceived as a personal and secluded work, a way of thinking that occupied my life for six years. I am most grateful to John Corrie for his support and encouragement during this time.

There are many people who have assisted in my research. I am indebted to Byron Harvey, who showed me the Southwest he knows so deeply and with whom I spent many hours analyzing basket technique and design; to Gary Shaffer, who took time to instruct me in the Navajo language; to Pam Logan, who cared for my children during field work; and to Elizabeth Zelvin, who edited the final manuscript.

Much of the Pomo material was given me by Bob Jackson, who believes in his heritage, and that, perhaps, some small segment of it can be recorded in this way. He has inspired me to believe likewise.

I would like to express my appreciation to the Museum of Navaho Ceremonial Art in Santa Fe, which supported my field work on the Navajo Reservation for three summers, and especially to its director, Bertha Dutton.

Finally, let me acknowledge my husband, Daniel, whose photographic contribution makes this book truly a joint effort.

Introduction

I HAVE TRAVELED through Arizona, New Mexico, Utah and California, sitting on the earth, in modern kitchens and in meeting houses, weaving many kinds of baskets. The types selected here do not represent all the basket weaving tribes of America today, nor all the techniques, such as plaiting, twilling, twining and coiling, but a selection was made on the basis of my immediate expertise.

Each tribe produces a basket suited to its social, religious and geographical environment. But cultural traits are in a constant state of flux. The basket changes in design, form and function as the culture's attitude toward it changes. This does not necessarily mean quality is threatened. The Pima basket may have been purely utilitarian in its many forms and techniques, but the miniatures, beaded baskets and *ollas* (Spanish term for a globular, widemouthed jar) woven for the tourists and collectors are fine examples of the art. The Navajo "wedding basket" used in sings has remained static for over a hundred years, yet some peripheral design experimentation has taken place in parts of the reservation, even though these new baskets are not acceptable for religious purposes.

This indigenous change is true in the weaving of most peoples. I believe that it is more important that a strength of culture, a sign of lineage be kept, rather than a stubborn purity maintained. Individual expression has always been encouraged. Although baskets are quite easily recognized as belonging to one tribe or another, the weaver herself makes small variations: she may increase the number of stitches in a design element, add a petal or two to the traditional squash blossom, or fill in a white space with a human or animal figure.

As most basket making is woman's work, the time spent weaving was interlaced with young children's play. In such an atmosphere deep friendship may easily develop between women of different cultures, as work and the care of children are basic concerns which affect our daily life.

I remember one afternoon at Navajo Mountain spent with a woman who spoke no English, and my Navajo was extremely rudimentary. We sat in the brush shelter with our materials soaking in a common white enamel bucket, silently working. I asked simple questions about color and design and preparation. She took my basket from my hands every now and then, laughing, with averted eyes, and showed it to her boy. I spoke haltingly of my sons; we continued to work, and only occasionally would we catch each other's eye and smile.

1: The Pomo Basket

Pika

I used to go to the top of that hill, Red Mountain, and look down . . . the valley was sure pretty . . . there was lots of trees then. Now there's too many houses.

MOLLIE JACKSON

HABITAT

THE TRADITIONAL LAND of the Pomo was the valley of the Russian River, the lake district around Clear Lake, and the coastal communities on the Pacific. Looking at a map of California, this territory extended northward from just above Bodega Bay to Fort Bragg, eastward to encompass Clear Lake, and south to swing just east of Santa Rosa.

The vegetation was luxuriant. In March the grasses were ready to eat. The Pomo picked all kinds of clover (*so*); dandelions (*ditsa so*); fiddleneck (*chimaa*); a celery-like plant called *shabuda;* angelica (*bachoa*); tule buds from Lake County; and, as always, ate corn mush (*t'oo*). They caught any available fish and hunted the yearling deer. April was the time of bulbs which were baked instead of eaten raw like the grasses. There were mission bells, blue dicks, cat-ears, Diogenes lantern, and the tops of the soapweed, well known also for the soaplike quality of its root.

"Everything was blooming in May," and it was also the beginning of the berry season: strawberry, blackberry, salmonberry, which lasted through July, and for the huckleberry and manzanita, through September. During June, July and August the people "moved toward the coast to gather their stuff for the winter," and generally to have a festive time camping on the beach.

Crab (*k'ii*), abalone (*t'im*), mussel (*k'al*), sea urchin (*kat'ik*), the black china slipper (*kataa*) and the larger red one (*muum*), surf fish (*tchusha*), eel (*bawol*), and kelp were caught, and either eaten then and there or dried for winter storage.

On the way back inland in September and October the nut gathering took place. The most prized acorns were from the tan oak (*bidu*) and the black oak, and supplied the chief diet of not only the Pomo, but most of the Indian peoples of northern California. July through November deer were hunted.

During the winter months, November to March, everything that had been gathered in previous months was eaten and it was "time for a woman to sit around and do nothing — to make baskets."

The Pomo culture now hangs by a thread, and this thread is the warp and weft of the Pomo basket. Yet the plants which supplied the fiber for these baskets are no longer plentiful.

The land has been dramatically changed. Valleys in which there were homes, camping grounds and whole villages, from which the *Hintil* (the Pomo people) set off to fish the rivers and lakes, have been flooded. Or the land has been re-sown, the walking paths paved over into highways that bypass orchards and hopfields. When Mollie Jackson looked down over the Ukiah Valley fifty years ago, it was a different sight. The places of willow, sedge grass and redbud were guaranteed year after year. Now it is not only difficult to find new growth, but exhausting for the old women to think of traveling to unknown areas.

The scarcity of correct plants is one reason that fewer Pomo baskets are being made. The second reason is that the young girls are simply not interested. But whether or not basket making is a dying art, it should, above all, be thought of as an art, and the right attention given — now.

HISTORY

IT HAS BEEN ESTIMATED that the ancient population of the Pomo did not exceed 8,000.* Their numbers were relatively stable at the time of contact in the early nineteenth century when the Russians came into California. Relations between the Pomo and the Russian explorers seem to have been good at first, but did not remain so, and with the subsequent movement of Spanish missions into northern California, and finally the enormous numbers of men who came in the gold rush days of the mid-1800's, the Pomo population dwindled.

At no time were the Pomo a united tribe, like the Pima and Navajo of Arizona, but lived together in small bands. Even communication was not always possible as there were seven dialects spoken, all belonging to the larger Hokan linguistic family, but nonetheless distinct enough to cause difficulty in understanding. Today, after moving from place to place following the hop harvest or grape and fruit picking seasons for several generations, two families living side by side may say of each other, "They speak different, they're from Cloverdale." It is more convenient to speak English, and as a result of pressure from the compulsory boarding schools, and the general loss of cul-

*A. L. Kroeber, *Handbook of the Indians of California,* Bulletin 78 of the Bureau of American Ethnology (Washington, D.C., 1925), p. 237.

tural adhesives such as ritual dances, families speak English even amongst themselves.

The main political organization is the Mendo-Lake Pomo Council, located in Ukiah. It serves the needs of the separate *rancherias* in Mendocino and Lake Counties. Lake County has seven *rancherias* (some were terminated in 1954, some were always privately owned): Sugarbowl; Big Valley; Upper Lake, divided into two sections, Hardesty and Duell; Ribinson; Sulphur Bank; Lower Lake; and Middletown. Mendocino County has four *rancherias:* Potter Valley; Hopland; Ukiah; and Pinoleville.

The people at Pinoleville, where I have often stayed, remain an independent group, both economically and socially. There are seventeen families there, ranging in age from a young child to a seventy-eight-year-old woman. Most of the men have jobs and feel strongly against taking welfare or any form of federal funding. Not many of the families are related. Although there have been marriages outside this local group of Pomo, it is felt that alliances to other tribes may bring about a certain dissension in political attitudes — a fracturing of the sense of community that was present in the old days. Geographic unity is disturbed by the necessity for employment in cities as far away as San Francisco and Los Angeles. But the family home is always open to a returning child or grandchild.

Pinoleville *rancheria* was terminated in 1954, and the Pomo now own their own homes, which are interspersed with white-owned vineyards and trailers. But the high land behind Pinoleville was always *Hintil* land, and will continue unmarked, as a legacy. Through these hills runs the old road to the coast by which the summer migration from the inland valley took place every year. Now the men drive this same way to go fishing.

USES

POMO WEAVING is unusual in that exceptionally fine work is done by Pomo weavers in both coiling and twining. Coiling is reserved for the making of gift baskets and showpiece works which are made to be burned at funeral ceremonies, while twining is the medium of a wide variety of culinary and storage baskets. Nearly all of these are decorated with designs except for openwork baskets. The Pomo are located near the boundary of a large block of tribes to the north and up the northwest coast, who practice twining exclusively, and to the south another large block who employ both techniques.

Although the Pomo use both techniques with equal care, they concentrate their fullest skill in the coiled gift baskets. These are often covered, on every other stitch, by feathers: red from the woodpecker scalp, yellow from the meadowlark, dull red from the robin's breast, blue from the California jay, and green from the mallard. Feathers from the topknot of the quail may be placed at intervals around the rim, or scattered about the surface.

But it is in the twined basketry of the Pomo that the processes of everyday life are most clearly seen. Men do the coarser work, such as baby baskets, traps, and wood carrying baskets; the women make the many baskets used in grinding the acorn for *t'oo* or acorn soup. The Yurok chapter explains the twining techniques in detail, but here I will describe the *t'oo* making, to evoke a sense of the culinary style of the northern California Indian, which still surfaces among the Pomo, the Yurok and other people on occasion.

All the old, much used baskets are brought out of storage, the pounding stone set in a shady place, and the steady thud of pestle on dried acorns is heard. It is early morning. The whole day will be taken up with the activity. In the fall acorns were gathered in the twined red and tan conical burden baskets. They were brought home and a winnowing basket was used to remove the inner skin: the acorns were rubbed together, loosening the skin, the basket shaken in a windy spot and the skins blown away.

Whatever skin still adheres is now rubbed off. To pound the acorns into fine meal, a *micha* — a deep basket with flaring sides, its bottom cut out — is placed over a round indented stone. The woman sits with her legs stretched straight out in front of her over the top of the basket to keep it steady. She puts the acorns in this basket and pounds them with a stone or metal pestle till a fine meal is produced. Another shallow basket, *dela,* is placed beside the mortar stone to collect this meal.

Acorns contain tannic acid, which is slightly poisonous and must be leached from the meal before cooking. A more openwork twined basket called *shakun* is used for this. Today, material like cheesecloth is laid in the *shakun,* the meal placed in this, and water poured through for about three hours. The old way was to scoop a hole out of the sand near the river and just lay the meal in this, basting with water, which ran into the ground.

When the meal tastes good and sweet, it is boiled in water without salt until it reaches the proper consistency. Cooking baskets were finely twined, and decorated in delicate patterns of redbud. Hot stones were held continuously in the cooking mush to facilitate boiling. Now the modern pot is used exclusively. Smaller replicas of the cooking basket were made for use as drinking cups and individual food servers.

MATERIALS

COMMON NAME	SCIENTIFIC NAME	POMO	USE
Willow	*Salix* sp.	*kalal*	warp
Sedge grass	*Carex barbarae*	*ka-hum*	weft
Redbud	*Cercis occidentalis*	*milay*	weft
Bulrush	*Scirpus pacificus*	*tsu-wish*	weft

Gathering: Time and Place

The SEDGE GRASS ROOTS are at their best in the fall of the year, about October. The women from Ukiah have a special place along the Eel River. Mollie Jackson told me she was having a picnic with her husband many years ago, and she looked over near the bank of the river and saw sedge grass growing. They were good roots and she has returned to this one place year after year, thinning out the roots and being delighted with their length and color. Any good sandy place along a river is suitable. And it is possible to cut these roots any time of the year as long as they are not old and dried out. What you must look for are long, new growths, the end of the roots still budding.

The WILLOW grows along the rivers and in low moist areas. The Pomo cut long new branches in the spring and fall. One of the species of willow used is a tree that grows by the Russian River, and another kind is more of a bush, the branches rising long and straight from the center at ground

Digging sedge grass roots

level. The white-leaved willow (*Salix argyrophylla*), prized for the coarse *shakun* basket, can also be used for the warp in the coiled basket. Any good pliable willow is acceptable. It should be chosen with three things in mind: it is a good length, the branch is straight, and the buds are very new and quite far apart to minimize the number of knots.

REDBUD is a small bush of the undergrowth which grows in the fairly dry climate of the inner coast ranges of California. The branches are cut in the fall, in the last days of October. At that time the bark will adhere, and as this is the part of the branch used to give the red color of the design, it is essential to cut at this time.

BULRUSH roots are collected in October. The brown root protrudes from a series of bulbs, and is cut in the manner described for the sedge grass. The two roots are structurally the same. (Few baskets are now made with this material as there is a scarcity in the familiar marshy places bordering Clear Lake where the weavers of Ukiah have been going for years.)

Method of Gathering and Preparing Materials

SEDGE GRASS ROOT

1. Dig the roots from the ground with a small garden fork. Even after finding the sedge grass, the roots are not so easy to locate, and care must be

Collecting the willow

taken, while digging, not to break the roots. Lengths of two or three feet are good. Bring home for further preparation.

2. Cut the two ends off.

3. Split the root in two while fresh. (See Pima method of willow splitting, p. 54.)

4. The parchment-like outer covering is stripped off by bending the root to make this bark stand up, and drawing the root its full length between your second and third fingers. It comes away easily.

5. Split the root again lengthwise.

6. These roughly prepared roots are now bent into a circle, as shown in the redbud section which follows. Let dry in the shade.

WILLOW

1. Cut the willow branch at its base.

2. The same day, strip off the bark as follows: A. At the butt end, strip back two or three strands of bark for about an inch. B. Wrap these tightly around and around the branch, exposing the white wood. C. Take the butt end between your teeth or hold with a cloth (the willow is slippery), grasp the twisted bark and pull hard toward the tip of the branch. All the

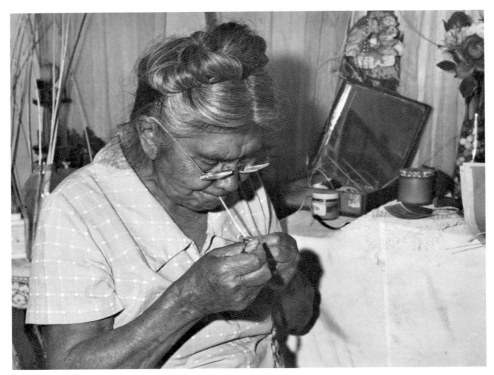

Splitting fresh sedge grass root

Mollie Jackson weaving. Note bundles of red and grey willow used for work baskets in foreground.

Redbud bundles for storage

bark will come off. Sometimes the willow is a bit dry and you will have to scrape it.

3. A piece of jagged broken glass is now used to whittle the willow withes down to an even size along the entire length. Hold the glass in the palm of your hand, and pass it over the willow as it runs between the third and fourth fingers.

4. Sandpaper gives a final smooth finish, and may be used exclusively for the evening up process if broken glass is not available or appears to be a rather frightening procedure.

5. The willow is stored in a dry place, tied according to categories of thickness. Only one size willow rod is used in a basket, to ensure uniformity of coil size.

REDBUD

1. Cut the redbud at its base. The bark is left on.

2. Split the branch in half lengthwise.

3. The same day, while the redbud is moist, split lengthwise again to remove the pith. What remains is the outer layer, fairly thin, but not fully prepared for weaving.

4. Bundles of redbud are tied up with the usual rag-string, and left to dry.

BULRUSH ROOT

This root is brown and needs to be dyed either when fresh or dried, to attain the rich black color of the design.

1. Keeping the roots whole, soak in a solution of water and rusty nails for several weeks. Experience will prove how long is needed before the desired shade is acquired. The dye solution may contain "black walnuts, rusty nails and ashes,"* or "the juice of the poison oak."†

2. Store in bundles either whole or split once in half lengthwise.

MAKING THE BASKET

Tools

AWL. You may buy this in a hardware store, and grind down the last inch to a finer point suitable for Pomo work. Or you may make your own awl of a needle set in wood. A No. 18 yarn darning needle or a No. 13 tapestry needle is recommended.

KNIFE. My teacher used a very small penknife that fit easily in the palm of the hand to whittle down the sides of the sedge grass root and redbud. A large knife is needed for gathering the materials.

BOWL. This is always used for soaking the materials.

GLASS. A piece of broken glass is

*Elsie Allen, *Pomo Basketmaking* (Healdsburg, Calif.: Naturegraph Publishers, 1972), p. 20.

†O. T. Mason, *Aboriginal American Basketry,* Annual Report of the Smithsonian Institution, 1902, p. 445.

Bullrush root

Tools: awl, knife and broken glass

used to scrape the willow. It is of irregular size and just fits the hand.

Method

All the materials must be soaked for about fifteen minutes in warm water before the final preparation.

This section includes further preparation of materials, as the final splitting is done just before or during the actual weaving. In other words, materials are generally stored in a semi-prepared state. Traditionally, the mother or grandmother, teaching the young girl, would prepare the materials for her at first.

SEDGE GRASS ROOTS

1. Split the roughly prepared root again to make the thin smooth sewing splint. Repeat the process as for the initial splitting, holding the root in your teeth and taking out the inner pithy core.

2. At this point, the edges of the root are still wavy. Even these out by holding the damp root in your left hand while you draw the knife down the entire length, a short distance at a time, moving the root through your hand as you do so. Do this on both edges.

3. The Pomo weaver uses a most ingenious method for "shining up" the root. Take a piece of discarded core section from the splitting process you have just finished, loop this piece over the root, draw it tight, and run

Shaving down sides of the sedge grass root

it back and forth over the root till little fibers come off. This action really smoothes out the *ka-hum*. Shape the end to make the needle point.

REDBUD

This material is thinned down exactly the same way just described for the root. Omit the shining up process. Width should approximate that of the root, so that the stitches in the basket are even. Sharpen the end for the needle point.

BULRUSH ROOT

Repeat as above for redbud.

WILLOW

Soak the butt end for a few minutes. Sharpen this end to a point, as it will be stuck into the root bundle of the basket beginning.

Beginning the Basket

"Pika di tsaatin," the weaver says: "I am starting the basket." The word *pika* refers specifically to the coiled basket, of which there are two types: one-stick (*tsai*) and three-stick (*bam sibu*).

The beginning for both types is the same. But when it comes time to add the willow, the weaver adds three rods for *bam sibu* instead of only one, and continues to coil, catching only the top rod of the previous row, instead of passing over the single rod of the previous row as well as the rod in progress. The two techniques produce dissimilar effects. The one-stick basket has long, pointed stitches that give it a serrated quality and a certain elegance. The three-stick basket has the squared off rectangular look of most coiled basketry.

We will deal here with the one-stick.

1. Take three or four pieces of "rough" root, about six to eight inches long, from the storage bundle, and soak a few minutes.

2. Take them out of the water and just twist them around each other a few times.

3. Make a fairly tight knot in the middle.

4. Insert a long piece of prepared root between the strands at one side of the knot.

Beginning the basket: twisted sedge grass roots

5. Make a complete loop into the center of the knot and around to secure the blunt end of the sewing root.

6. Push all root ends, except sewing strand, to your left, and hold firmly in left hand.

7. Insert sewing root through center of knot, making a stitch around the twisted roots, and pull tight.

Making one loop through center with root

8. Continue to do this, placing each stitch exactly to the left of the preceding one. You are working *right to left* or *counterclockwise*.

9. Depending on how tight your knot is, you may or may not have to use the awl at this point to make a hole for the root strand.

10. Keep twisting the rough root lengths in your left hand to make a rope-like bundle.

11. After about eight stitches, the rough roots become bulky and one or two should be cut off.

12. Continue to coil, sticking the awl into the root bundle instead of the center of the knot. Always draw the sewing root through the hole made by the awl.

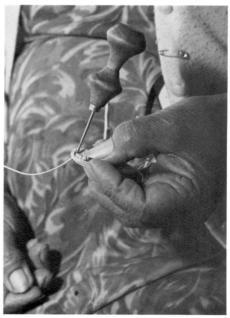

Making hole with awl

Coiling

Coiling

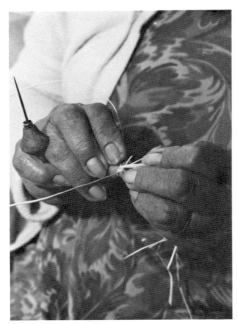

Coiling

One round completed

One round completed

13. Make one full round and a few more stitches, cutting off rough roots as necessary as you work along.

14. Cut off all remaining rough roots.

15. Add the sharpened willow that has been soaking in water by pushing the sharpened end into the bundle of roots, which, up to now, has been the foundation.

16. When you have made another round, this single rod will have become the foundation. Now you must make a hole with your awl below this rod (of the preceding row) so that each stitch will in fact be going around two rods, or two rows.

17. Roll the basket beginning on its edge to round the form.

18. Gaps appear between stitches as the basket increases in size. To keep the stitches tightly aligned, either put two stitches where only one would normally be, or split one stitch in two instead of placing the root between two stitches.

Remember to *keep all materials wet while working.*

Adding New Materials

1. To add a new piece of root when the old one becomes too short, make the usual hole with your awl and pull the root through this almost to the end.

2. Take the end facing you, and curve it back up and push under the

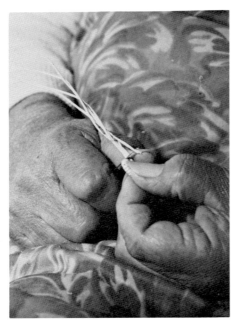

Cutting off roots

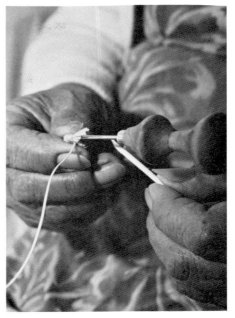

Making hole in center of roots in preparation for warp rod

Sharpening the willow for foundation rod

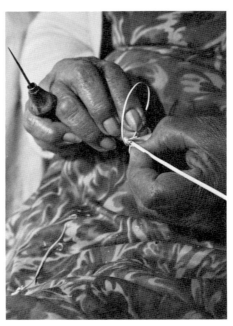

Adding willow rod as warp

rod of the new row. Hold this down with your left hand.

3. Continue the usual stitch, over the rod from the back, and through the hole in front, thus securing the end and completely hiding it.

4. The end of the old root is tucked into this stitch at the back, and cut off.

5. A new piece of willow is added when the foundation stick becomes perceptibly thinner. Break off the old stick and insert a new sharpened one.

6. Every now and then, as you proceed, gently pound the basket on a flat surface to keep it flat.

The design is started opposite the very first stitch at the center of the basket. Pomo weavers have always used only one color at a time in their baskets, either the red of the redbud or the black of the bulrush root. These materials are worked the same way as the root. Stitches in the design are counted for purposes of symmetry.

Form

The form of a Pomo basket is one of its most distinguishing characteristics. It curves outwards from the base and closes in at the lip rather like a very fine pot, and it is precisely this classical quality that is not present in

Pounding basket beginning with awl

Redbud is added for the design

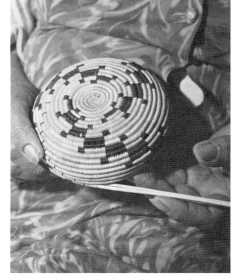

Whirlwind *design in a three-stick basket*

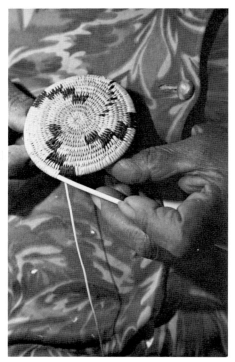

Beginning of whirlwind *design in redbud*
(*Note the pathway or* dau.)

Inside of same basket

the other basket types described. The Pima and Navajo weavers, making the open bowl-like basket, joke about the Pomo gift basket and say it is "inside out."

The same technique for shaping the basket is used in all instances. That is, the position of the foundaton (warp) bundle, or rod in this case, should lie exactly on top of the previous foundation if a flat surface is desired. This is done for the base of the Pomo basket. After approximately four rows of design have been made, the basket should start to curve outwards, and the foundation rod should now begin to rest slightly to the inside of the previous warp. (Note that this is exactly the opposite of the Pima and Navajo baskets.) With each row, feel the basket to be sure a smooth, even curve is forming. About three-quarters of the way through the design, the basket begins to curve inwards. Weave till the inner space feels enclosed, and the design has been completed.

The design in a Pomo coiled basket is woven to the rim, and is made of repetitive motifs which could, perhaps, end at any moment. Therefore be aware of the close relationship between the design and the form, for in the case of diagonal elements, the design ends as the form is complete.

Finishing Off

The design is completed, and one plain row made, tapering very gently to end at the point opposite the first stitch of the design. Gently shave down the willow rod, or, if using three rods, cut these down one at a time. An almost even top is greatly praised. A bump at the end may get a remark such as, "You were in a hurry."

DESIGN OF THE BASKET

MOST PEOPLE looking at an Indian basket design ask, "What is that called?" When I have asked this question of the weavers themselves, the reply is vague and uninterested, or if they ascribe definite names to certain elements, I feel they are repeating a description once given by an outsider. Not only are certain motifs particular to a tribe and have been as far back as memory, but the women accept these designs as part of the "being" of the basket. Designs are not laid on — or made up. They are an organic part of basket weaving, as they follow the form and technique.

Coiled basketry is, by definition, constructed in a circular manner. Some tribes weave in fairly static or banded designs; the Pomo are extraordinarily free in the variety of design types. They use horizontal, diagonal, crossing, radiating or isolated arrangements with equal ease. The effect is usually one of movement and flight.

Three-stick gift basket, partially covered with clam shell beads and feathers. The design is a variant of the complex motif arrowhead, *combined with the double band of rectangles called* ants. *Note that the design is woven to the last row, where it seems to move off the basket into space.*

Pomo design is further complicated by the use of beads and feathers. Beads were made from clam shells collected at Bodega Bay, ground down and pierced by the old hand-drill method. They were sewn in an apparently random way over the surface of the basket. On especially fine baskets, pendants of abalone shell, cut and weathered by the sea, are found. All these delicate white beads play off against the black and red designs.

So that the weaver may "see" her way around and around as she builds, she places a few separate stitches in a single line. Sometimes there is a break in the design; sometimes, no difference that I can see. This break or line is called the *dau* and is similar to the pathway in the Navajo basket.

I have drawn some of the design elements in the Pomo basket, and named them as I have been told. Others have already been written down in the descriptive literature. On flat paper, the triangles and steps seem simple enough. When woven in root and shades of red, they take in the light at separate moments, they curve, and form a complete basket.

Twined large storage basket of ti-stick *construction. The design in redbud is a variant of the common motif,* quail plumes.

2: The Yurok Basket

A-ka

While basket weaving sit with your back to the fire. Be cheerful. Do not think of it as hard work or the basket will not be good.

REA BARBER

HABITAT

THE YUROK are mountain people. They live back in the heavily wooded coastal hills of northern California between Eureka and Crescent City. It is truly remote territory, and can be reached by only three roads. One comes in from the east through the Karok villages of Happy Camp and Clear Creek. The second road is unpaved, and runs over the ridge to the ocean, is unpassable in the winter rains and snows, but is beautiful in autumn and spring, the high meadows yellow with grasses and the sky wide as you come up from the valley. The third route comes from the south, through Hoopa Valley. A small oasis of space amidst the continual mountains, this valley is eight miles long and is the main open area where the Hoopa have their homes and school and shops. At the northern end of the valley, the hills close in again, the Klamath River flows in from the north to join the Trinity, and at this confluence is the hamlet of Weitchpec — center of Yurok civilization.

As much as the Yurok love the mountains, they also love and depend on the river. Settlements run adjacent to the Klamath, and where it flows into the sea at Requa, the Yurok have continued their life along the coast. They are a fishing people and were once well known among the Karok and Hoopa for their skill at making the redwood dugout canoe. It was made for river use and not to go out upon the ocean. The men would content themselves with surf fishing and tell stories of mermaids who sat on large rocks off the coast.

The land is damp, and grows plant life which can hang onto a mountain side. There are several large ferns at lower altitudes near the coast, and towering over them the conifers, whose roots are the mainstay of the Yurok basket. Hazel switches grow easily by the houses and provide ready materials. The shiny sourgrass is burnt off the hilltops once a year to encourage good new growth the next. The alder and willow are still growing wild and untouched by the hands that have so altered the Pomo landscape. Porcupine quills were used in the basket in the past, but never in large quantities, and now, given the deadly hunting method of a fast car on the road at night, the odds are about even that if someone wants to use the quills, he can find a porcupine.

Food is repetitive but plentiful. The Yurok, along with their neighbors the Hoopa and Karok, like to eat acorn mush and deer meat, and all kinds of fish, especially the salmon. The old willow woven eel baskets have been duplicated in wire, and men go fishing as often as possible. The tables are set with packaged bread, milk, and hamburger, but the back porch is still littered with the baskets used in making acorn mush. They are hung up and collect cobwebs, acorns grow moldy in buckets, basketry materials lie around in every room as if the past were never interrupted, the men had never gone off to work in the sawmill, and the women had never forgotten the words of their language.

Because of the isolation, and because the rivers continue to flow, the people have kept much of their old character. They still think of direction in terms of the Klamath, "downstream" and "upstream," and the doors of all the houses face downstream.

HISTORY

THE YUROK cannot easily be isolated from their neighbors, the Hoopa and Karok, in that all three share a similar culture. But in their language they differ markedly. The Yurok are related to the eastern Algonquian linguistic family, the Hoopa are Athabascan, and the Karok are a northern unit of the Hokan group.

According to a census taken in 1852,* the Yurok numbered as many as the Hoopa and Karok combined. Population of the three groups declined from an overall figure of about 5,000 to 2,000 in 1910, the Yurok constituting 668 persons. These numbers show quite a high survival rate for California tribes, due in part to geographic isolation, lack of placer gold, and the fact that the Hoopa were established early on reservation land, and left alone. The Yurok remained on their old land, "downstream" along the Klamath, and the Karok "upstream."

These people did not roam far from the rich food supplies of the rivers, coast and hills. There was commerce, intermarriage and mild feuding between the Yurok, Hoopa and Karok, which continues to the present day. The Tribal Council is located in Hoopa Valley proper, where there is a modern school, tribal-owned gas station, motel, restaurant, and craft

*Kroeber, *Handbook,* p. 16.

shops. But the Yurok still prefer their mountainous terrain behind Weitch-pec, where house sites retain their name for generations, even after the people have died or left.

There are at the present time (1973) active basketry and language classes for both the Hoopa and Yurok. At Orleans, basketry is taught one night a week, and is open to students from junior high school age onwards. The teacher, a Hoopa/Yurok woman, is supported by the College of the Redwoods in nearby Eureka. Hoopa Valley has basket classes starting with the eight-year-old girl. "Downriver" at Johnsons, the Yurok conduct several evening classes each week. The materials used are the same for all, and as these are spread out over Hoopa and Yurok territory, it means that buying and selling can take place and a supply of materials be ensured. Design ownership is somewhat com-plicated, the Yurok claiming to in-fluence the Hoopa, for, according to Yurok weaver Rea Barber, "the old Hoopa basket making has been gone a long time."

This renewed interest in basket weaving has enabled the women to make extra money. Their baskets are sold at local church gatherings to peo-ple within the community, or outside, at Hoopa Valley craft shops to tour-ists, and are being seen more and more at Indian shows in other states. This suits the Yurok temperament

well. They are an individualistic peo-ple, concerned with prestige and ma-terial gain. There is no particular responsibility to community feeling, and no sense of betrayal of tribal tra-dition if a weaver copies an old basket. Baskets have always been items of barter. In this sense there can be a comparison drawn between the Yurok and Paiute weavers, who both have traditionally made baskets to sell outside the tribe, and as a result, work all year round, considering it digni-fied work.

At this point in time, it seems most likely that the Yurok/Hoopa/Karok complex of weavers will persist, due to a greater sympathy with the ma-terialistic values of the larger Anglo society. Nothing will be lost. Isolation of the valley will ensure a certain peace and non-interference, and the growing numbers of young people attending colleges in northern Cali-fornia will lead to a general climate of sophistication needed for dialogue and bargaining power. The people will weave baskets on their own terms.

USES

YUROK LIFE depended largely on the acorn harvest and the catch of fish that could be taken each year. Baskets were made to fit in with the needs of preparing and serving these foods. A description of the acorn process has

Acorn hopper

Storage basket, diameter 9″ height 17½″

Gambling tray, diameter 21″

been given in the Pomo chapter, and can be understood as being similar to the Yurok.

Following is a list of basket types, some of which are still in use today.

The BURDEN BASKET is a rather squat conical affair common throughout northern California. It was described to me as a "wood carrying basket," but seems also to be used as a picnic basket. It is simple open twining, perhaps decorated with a row of crossed warp towards the rim, which is finished off in a crude braid. Three leather straps are attached, coming together in one strap which passes across the forehead of the carrier.

A closely twined burden basket faced with sourgrass was used to carry acorns or seeds.

The HOPPER or acorn pounding basket was made in close twine with a simple design in sourgrass. The bottom was cut out, the basket placed over the·mortar stone, and a pestle used to pound the acorns to a fine meal.

The STORAGE BASKET was globular with a slightly constricted neck. The surface, covered with sourgrass, often had a design of isosceles triangles and oblique parallelograms created by leaving the weft, or root, exposed.

A large TRAY up to two feet in diameter was used for sifting the acorns in a fashion similar to the Pomo. It is faced with sourgrass, the exposed weft creating radiating or banding motifs.

A smaller, more coarsely woven close twine tray is put beside the woman pounding acorns, in order to catch the fine meal. A finely woven, more elaborate tray was used for gambling games.

A shallow open twine tray, approximately a foot in diameter, was used to sift and sort berries.

A SIFTER of open weave is used to separate the fine from the coarse acorns as they are prepared.

Acorn mush was made in a COOKING BASKET shaped like a large bowl with fairly straight sides. Simple designs in sourgrass were used only on the upper body, the lower third being simple twine in the root.

The individual ACORN BOWL or *porcheks* is a smaller version of the cooking basket.

A round MAT or *hoh-a'lak,* covered with a leaf, was used to serve fish or berries.

The EEL TRAP was made of unpeeled sticks, and was about five or six feet long. These traps are now made of wire, but construction is the same.

The Yurok HAT is the epitome of grace and fine workmanship. For this the maidenhair fern is used extensively. One could "wear it anytime," Rea Barber says, "if you're rich enough to have it." They were custom made for sale, and were highly prized. Work hats were worn around the house and for protection against the

Berry sifting tray

HEARD MUSEUM COLLECTION

*Cooking basket, diameter 8¼",
height 7½"*

HARVEY FINE ARTS COLLECTION, HEARD MUSEUM

*Individual eating bowl, diameter 5",
height 3"*

Hat, diameter 6¾", height 4"

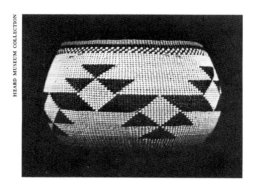

Bowl, diameter approximately 6", height approximately 4"

Tobacco basket, diameter 4", height 4"

weight of the burden basket strap. The dress hat is distinguished from the work hat in that the former has a flat top and only touches the head at the rim, and the latter is dome-like and fits the head snugly.

The MEDICINE BASKET was made for cooking medicine and was the same size as the hat. Dark maidenhair fern was not used.

The medicine man kept his herbs in an HERB BASKET similar to the hat, but this also lacked the maidenhair fern decoration.

A BOWL was made for general household use. It was covered over the entire surface with sourgrass, and could be as elaborate as the hat. The form differed in that the bowl turned inwards slightly at the rim.

Rather grotesque GOBLET forms have been made since the 1920's. Intricate in material and details, they are made to show off skill and appeal to the tourist.

Kroeber cites the *rumitsek* or openwork globular basket used for holding spoons and odds and ends.* Much in evidence today in Yurok homes is an openwork twine slab with woven pockets one above the other. These receptacles are hung on the wall, and collect oddments and family treasures.

The BABY BASKET or *key-woy* is still very popular among the Yurok mothers, and is a pleasing tourist object.

*Kroeber, *Handbook*, p. 89.

Anybody can make the basket for the baby, and it is considered an honor "to be sleeping in your basket."* Sex differentiations are made thus: the girl's basket has a wider bottom and is decorated with dentalia at the top sides; a boy's has tassels and a bow and arrow hanging from the sides. A new baby basket is made as the child grows — he may have as many as four during his first year.

Tobacco was kept in a small, globular lidded TOBACCO BASKET in sourgrass overlay with simple design. "A few old Yurok were passionate smokers, but the majority used tobacco moderately. The native Nicotianas are rank, pungent, and heady."†

A variation on this tobacco basket is the more modern TRINKET BASKET with handled lid. The elaborate one illustrated (p. 48) might contain "shell money, beads, woodpecker crests, carved rocks and obsidian blades etc."‡

*Ibid.

†Ibid.

‡Lila O'Neale, *Yurok-Karok Basket Weavers,* University of California Publications, American Archaeology and Ethnology, vol. 32 (1932), p. 42.

A variety of baskets in a Yurok house

MATERIALS

COMMON NAME	SCIENTIFIC NAME	YUROK	USE
Maidenhair fern	*Adiatum pedatum*	*rek-goh*	weft
Hazelnut	*Corylus californica*	*hoo-lih*	warp
Sourgrass/Squawgrass	*Xerophyllum tenax*	*haam-aw*	weft
Sugar pine	*Pinus lambertiana*		weft
Yellow pine	*Pinus ponderosa*	*waah-peh*	weft
Giant chain fern	*Woodwardia spinulosa*	*pa-ap*	weft
White alder (bark)	*Alnus rhombifolia*		dye (weft)
Red alder (roots)	*Alnus oregana*		weft
Willow	*Salix* sp.	*paxkwo*	warp, weft

Gathering: Time and Place

The Yurok weaver has the HAZELNUT sticks literally at her doorstep. She may plant her own bush behind the house and cut when ready. This is done from early April through May. As hazelnut occurs over most of the northern two-thirds of the state of California, finding this bush should provide no problem. If necessary very thin willow sticks can be substituted.

The women used to burn the ground in summer or fall so that the hazel would grow in straight the following spring. The sticks were left another year, and were then cut the second spring when they were from twelve to thirty-six inches high.

SOURGRASS or SQUAWGRASS is a greenish-yellow finely serrated grass. Distribution is from northern California up through western Oregon and Washington to Vancouver Island. In the vicinity of Hoopa Valley, it is found in the high meadows between the Yurok settlements and the coast. Picked in spring, from the middle of April through July, the old growth is then burnt off so that next year's crop will have room to grow well. Choose grass growing in the shade: it is not brittle and bleached out.

A variety of CONIFER ROOTS are used for the weft of the Yurok basket. Merrill cites the use of coast redwood (*sequoia sempervirens*), juniper (*Juniperus occidentalis*), digger pine (*Pinus sabiniana*).* My teacher told me she sometimes uses the root of willow, cottonwood, red alder and spruce. The common characteristic of all these tree roots is a strength and pliability that will allow ease in ma-

*Ruth E. Merrill, *Plants Used in Basketry by the California Indians* (Ramona, Calif.: Acoma Books, 1970), appendix.

nipulating the weft back and forth around the stiff warp.

Dig up the root any time, but March seems favored by the Yurok, and reflects an impatience to get back to collecting materials after a winter's seclusion.

RED ALDER / WILLOW / COTTONWOOD roots are cut at the edge of a river where high water has washed away the sand, exposing the roots. These may be three to six feet long.

From mid-summer (June) and into the fall, as late as mid-October, the MAIDENHAIR FERN is ready. Yurok women travel to the coast where the fern grows in great quantities beneath the conifers, dampened by perpetual sea mists. The ferns also grow inland, high up on creek beds in the Karok region. Distribution and use in basketry extends from Mendocino County in California along the Pacific to southern Alaska.

The WOODWARDIA FERN is a woodland species, like the maidenhair, and grows in moist soil and shade. Rea Barber suggests that it should be allowed to grow all summer and picked in the fall or winter months when it is "not so easy to break." But it can be picked in June and July, although at that time a certain woody substance clings to the inner strands, making preparation more difficult.

WHITE ALDER grows locally around Weitchpec and Hoopa Valley. The inside of the bark is used as a red dye,

and is taken off the tree any time of the year.

Method of Gathering and Preparing Materials

HAZEL STICKS

1. Cut and strip bark off the hazel branches as described under WILLOW PREPARATION in the Pomo and Pima chapters.

2. Dry for several days.

3. The Yurok weaver then sorts these stocks into four piles, graded according to length and thickness: a bundle of six inch sticks, one of ten inch sticks, etc. These are then tied up for storage.

Prepared basketry materials, l. to r.: two bundles of graded hazel sticks, maidenhair fern stalks, sourgrass bundle, partially prepared conifer root, split conifer root

Woodwardia spinulosa, *giant chain fern*

Pounding woodwardia stem with rock

Twisting woodwardia stem to separate outer section from inner filaments

SOURGRASS

1. Nip off the grass at the bottom of each stalk, taking pieces from the center of the clump.

2. Dry in the sun for three days.

3. Tie into bundles of similar width, as you did for the hazel sticks.

CONIFER ROOT

1. Dig the root out of the ground. It will be about three or four feet long and as thick around as your forearm.

2. Bake or boil whole till the skin falls off.

3. Split into four sections.

4. Then split lengthwise into long thin strips about one-quarter to one-half inch wide.

5. Store looped over and tied.

RED ALDER/WILLOW/COTTONWOOD

Willow root may be split at once, but it is often the correct size as found. Alder and cottonwood roots may need to be split lengthwise till they approximate the size of the conifer.

MAIDENHAIR FERN

1. Pick frond at base of stalk, and strip off leaflets.

2. Tie these stalks loosely, and store upright in a dark, dry place. It is advised to wrap the ferns in newspaper as sunlight will fade them.

WOODWARDIA FERN

1. The fern is picked at the base of the stalk and the top and leaflet taken off as for maidenhair.

2. Pound vigorously with a rock on the flatter side of the stem.

3. Twist back and forth to separate outer section of stalk.

4. Take out the two leathery light green strands inside the stalk.

5. Discard outer section.

6. The two strands are dried and then dyed with the alder bark.

WHITE ALDER

The bark of this tree produces the red dye mentioned above. In the old days, the weaver would chew the bark and simply pass the woodwardia strands through this dye bath in her mouth to give them the red color.

1. Pound the inside layer of bark.

2. Put in water and bring to the boil. (Some weavers use only cold water, saying heat destroys the material.)

3. Add the dried woodwardia strands and steep in the solution till the right color is obtained.

4. Take strands out and put in plastic bag or wrap in white cloth, till the color sets.

5. Dry quickly in the sun.

MAKING THE BASKET

Tools

AWL. In twined basketry, the awl is used only for pushing the stitches closer together. Among skilled weavers, hands and teeth do the major work here.

KNIFE. This is now used to scrape the root, but you may enjoy trying the traditional *mussel shell.*

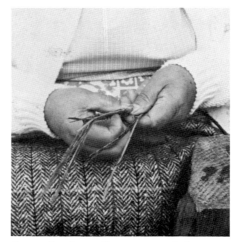

Separating inner filament strands from outer section of woodwardia stem

Taking the inner filament strands from the woodwardia stem

The outer section is discarded and the two inner filaments of the woodwardia fern are dried in preparation for dyeing

KINDLING WOOD. A piece of wood, split two inches lengthwise, is used to press the maidenhair fern.

BOWL. The usual large bowl for soaking materials is required.

Method

All materials must be soaked in hot water for about fifteen minutes before final preparation.

HAZEL STICKS

1. Soak for a few minutes.

2. Chew an inch at the butt end, making the stick pliable before starting the basket, and before each stick is added from then on. Or you may crush the ends lightly with a rock.

CONIFER ROOTS

1. Boil for fifteen minutes at least before final splitting.

2. Scrape with a long sweeping movement over the entire length with a dull knife (or mussel shell) to soften. This takes some time, but finally smaller fibers will break away.

3. Split these fibers into finer strips with your fingernail. Uniformity in width and thickness is desired. Remember, for much of the basket, this root will be overlaid with another material, and therefore should not be too bulky. The strips should be about one-sixteenth inch wide.

SOURGRASS

1. These strands, if sorted well beforehand, are fairly uniform in size

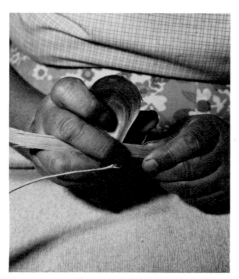

Scraping conifer root with mussel shell

and can be used as is, after a few minutes soaking.

2. For finer work, split in two. Be careful handling this material as the edge can cut if dry.

MAIDENHAIR FERN

1. Split the stem in two, either while fresh, or after dampening subsequent to storage.

2. Soak about an hour, as this material is brittle and breaks easily.

3. Split by pulling the fern stem through the kindling wood tool, pressing hard with your hand as you run the wood over the entire fern length. There is a natural edge line which should be observed if possible.

4. Run your fingernail along the break created by the tool pressure, and pull apart into two sections.

5. Discard the rubbery inner strands. The red side is not used except by the most thrifty weavers as it breaks too easily.

6. Even out any irregularities in width with your fingernail.

7. Split again in half if a thinner piece is desired.

(A beginner's basket certainly does not need this fern, and to avoid frustration, I would suggest using it only when the weaver is quite skilled in twining.)

WOODWARDIA FERN

Soak a few minutes before using.

Beginning the Basket

Note that twining is from left to right or clockwise, and that materials are kept wet while working. Remember to hold the work taut while beginning the basket.

1. Place two hazel sticks together, butt ends overlapping three or four inches.

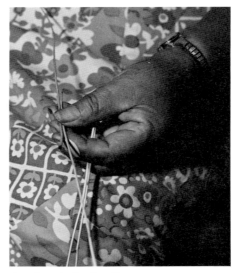

Starting the basket, Step 1

Starting the basket, Step 2

Starting the basket, Step 3

2. Wrap conifer root around at center, holding one end in your mouth and the other in your right hand.

3. Lay two more sticks on top of root held in right hand.

4. Exchange root in mouth for one held in hand by passing over these two sticks.

5. Repeat Steps 3 and 4.

6. Give sticks a half-turn; they are now horizontal to your body.

7. Place two sticks on top of and perpendicular to the four sticks.

8. Pass root over sticks as in Step 4.

9. Repeat Steps 7 and 8 twice.

10. Weave around corner, passing root over each pair of sticks lying horizontal to your body.

11. Continue to twine one round, over and under two sticks.

The first stick, or starting point, is called the *noor*. Mark this stick with a magic marker, as it must be observed on each round.

Starting the basket, Step 4

Starting the Basket, Step 7

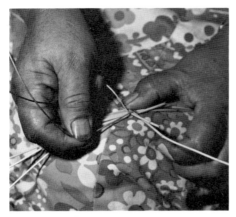

Starting the basket, Step 8

Starting the basket, Step 9

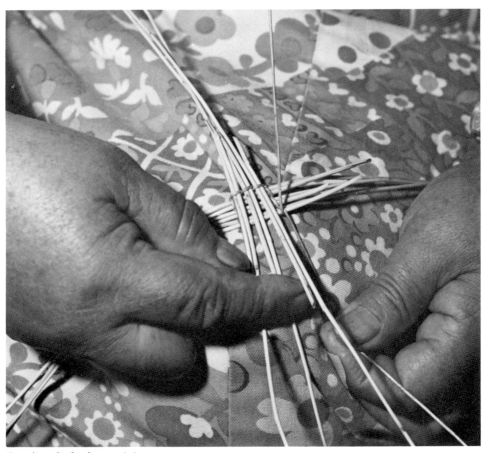

Starting the basket: twining

Three-strand twining

Adding a stick at the corner

Rea Barber told me, "Always finish to your *noor* or your mind becomes unstable, and you will not be thinking all the time to gain a better life — your mind becomes *ei-ge'athl* or 'just anyway.' If the *noor* is not reached when the basket is laid down, angels from under the ground will come up and dance on it and make it no good."

Adding New Materials

1. Two sticks after the *noor* is reached, add another piece of root. Just put the root in the interstices between the other two roots. You will now be twining with three roots, a technique known as *three-strand twine*.

2. Go around once with the three-strand twine technique, as follows: A. Root at the farthest left, facing weaver, moves over stick to its immediate right; root which has been lying behind moves under this and comes forward between the next stick. B. The same position as before is now attained, i.e., one root is to the back of the work, and two roots are to the front.

3. Go around once again, being especially careful at the corners, as the gap makes twining rather tricky.

4. Add a stick at the corner, to the left of the first stick. They are considered as one stick in this round, and woven together.

5. Twine one round, adding one stick at each corner.

6. Twine one round without adding sticks.

7. Change twining technique: go back to two roots over two sticks, known as *diagonal weaving*. Just drop the middle root at the back of the work.

8. On this round, you may have to add a stick at each corner to shorten gap.

9. Next round, add a stick every other stick all the way around.

10. Make one plain row (do not add sticks).

11. Repeat Steps 9 and 10 till you are eight rounds from the beginning.

12. On this round you may add some overlay design. Place a dampened strand of sourgrass over one of the root wefts. Make sure not to twist the weft strands as root and sourgrass pass together behind the sticks, as the sourgrass design must not show on the back, or inside, of the Yurok basket. When adding the sourgrass, place the smooth side uppermost; back of sourgrass has a slightly raised line running the length of the strand.

You will now have an alternating pattern: one root plain, one root overlaid by grass.

Overlay design with maidenhair fern

13. Continue to add overlay for several rounds to form a design.

14. At the *noor* return to the three-strand twine for one round. Use just the root, simply cutting off the grass at the back of the work.

15. Twine one more round, adding sticks evenly every other stick. This marks the end of the bottom of the basket. No more new sticks will be necessary after the basket begins to curve.

When a stick becomes too short, add a new one next to it in the manner described for increasing.

Care must be taken that the weft strands are the same width. Uneven widths can cause the work to buckle.

The awl is used only to push the stitches firmly down onto the preceding round. This should be done with your thumb as you twine, pushing at the back of the work. If you see gaps appearing between rounds, use the awl.

Form

The correct Yurok hat, trinket or cooking basket shape is attained by holding the basket close to the body and forcing the sticks slightly inward as you work. As no sticks are added after the main design element is started, the basket quite naturally follows its curve on a stable number of warp. The sides of the basket should be practically straight.

Finishing Off

The sticks are cut off flush with the last round. Work is tight enough to keep the basket from unravelling. Wire cutters may be used to cut off the sticks, as well as all excess materials on the inside.

DESIGN OF THE BASKET

AS I SIT writing this in the desert, a Yurok hat on the table in front of me, I look, and remember so well the tight and complex mountain life of the Yurok people, the running of their rivers, and the small sky. All this landscape is in the hat. Black marks set against a light backdrop like tree tops in individual play against a pale sky, and bands and parallelograms like dark rivers and houses fixed to the sloping earth.

The Yurok weavers, who live locked in place, repeat the old designs again and again. Experimentation is not encouraged, but a certain respect is shown a weaver who is technically skilled and can "make up" a design. Too much elaboration is not pleasing; large areas of unbroken color and good spacing make more sense.

A favorite design or "mark," the oblique parallelogram, is called *flint,* and is the basic element in the majority of baskets. The flint may be broken by the internal use of such elements as the snake, stripes, or triangular insets. It is used in all kinds of baskets, from the work baskets, where it appears in a bold and undecorated manner, to the hats and fancy baskets in which the flint is elaborated upon by internal rhythms.

The weaver observes rules of design in making hats, especially the dress hat. The hat is divided into three zones: A. Area from the center or start to the three-strand twine at the turn — this design must be congruous with the main mark. B. Area from the three-strand twine to the end of the banding or row of three-strand twine — within this area falls the main mark in three or four units. C. Area from the three-strand twine to the edge — may be a different design from the first area, but must be altogether harmonious.*

Unlike the dress hats, fancy baskets have no prescribed zones and may or may not satisfy the Yurok rules of perfection. Experimentation can take place without censure. Illustrated is a modern lidded trinket basket, that may have evolved out of the lidded storage basket. It still retains the traditional *wax'poo* mark, and conforms to specifications of tradition in this way. But the form is awkward, and lacks the simple lines, for instance, of the old tobacco basket on page 30.

Weaving skill is considered a gift, and certain women in each genera-

*O'Neale, p. 67.

tion have been known to make the best baskets. They sell well. If a weaver needs cash quickly, she may just sit down for three days and turn out a small basket. The women have a number of "starts" lying around their houses. This allows a buyer a choice of colors and design; it also alleviates the boredom of working on only one basket.

These starts can be made without the overlay in grass or they can be as elaborate as the weaver feels is possible, considering compatibility with the main mark.

The starts are beautiful as is, and you may want to stop there, making a miniature basket or flat tray to demonstrate twining ability, or add your mark in the way of Yurok basket making.

Plain basket start in conifer root

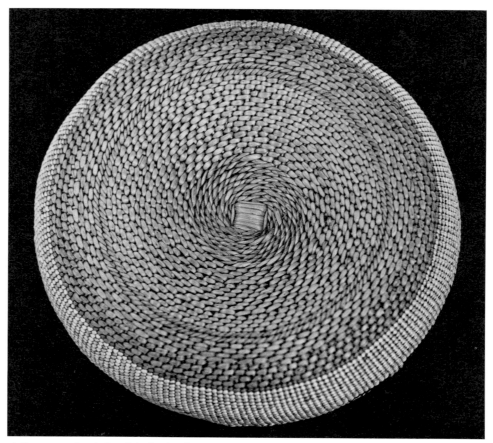

A fine example of the plain basket bottom in conifer root showing both two-strand and three-strand twining. Note the number of rows made before the main overlay weaving begins.

Start of basket using alternating overlays in sourgrass and maidenhair fern. Note the three rows in which plain root and sourgrass overlay alternate.

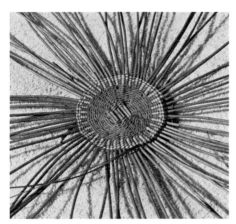

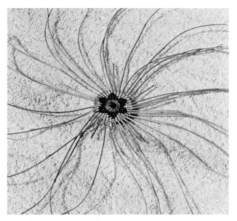

Basket start showing different weaves: first eight rows are three-strand twine in plain root; next three rows are two-strand twine in alternating root and sourgrass overlay; next two rows are two-strand twine in sourgrass overlay; last row is two-strand twine in dyed woodwardia fern.

Basket start suitable for miniature or medallion. Dark design is woodwardia fern dyed with alder bark; light area is sourgrass overlay.

Partially completed basket with flint *design in sourgrass and maidenhair fern overlay*

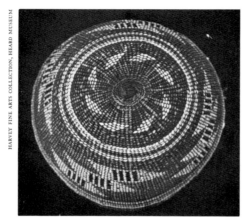

Old hat, flint *design, diameter 7",
height 3½"*

Old hat, flint *design with* ladder. *Note the
three zones. Diameter 7", height 4"*

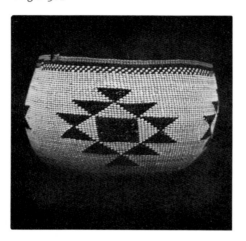

*Trinket basket. Start is three-strand twine
in plain root; then three rows in alternating
sourgrass and maidenhair fern overlay;
bottom is completed in sourgrass overlay;
then two rows in three-strand twine in
plain root; main body is two-strand twine
in sourgrass overlay with* sit down *design
in maidenhair fern; border repeats bottom
motif; last two rows are in plain root.*

Example of complex design on bottom of Yurok basket; start is three-strand twine in plain root; next three rows are two-strand twine; then two rows three-strand twine; three rows two-strand twine. (Note at this point that sticks are added all the way around for increasing size, and the alternation of woodwardia fern and plain root is begun.) The basket proceeds in five rows of two-strand twine (warp sticks are again added evenly); two rows three-strand twine; one row two-strand twine in plain root.

Zig-zag design starts in the sourgrass overlay against dyed woodwardia fern; then two rows in maidenhair fern; and the main body design continues in sourgrass and maidenhair overlay against the dyed woodwardia fern.

HEARD MUSEUM COLLECTION

Modern lidded trinket basket, a variation of the traditional wax′poo *design*

Fine example of a complex bottom of Yurok basket. Start is three-strand twine in plain root; next four rows are two-strand twine in maidenhair fern overlay; then foot *design variation in fern against sourgrass overlay background; bottom is completed in one row plain root in three-strand twine, three rows fern, two rows sourgrass and two rows fern overlay. These last seven rows are worked in two-strand twine which continues into the main design on the body of the basket. Diameter 6½″, height 3¾″*

3: The Pima Basket

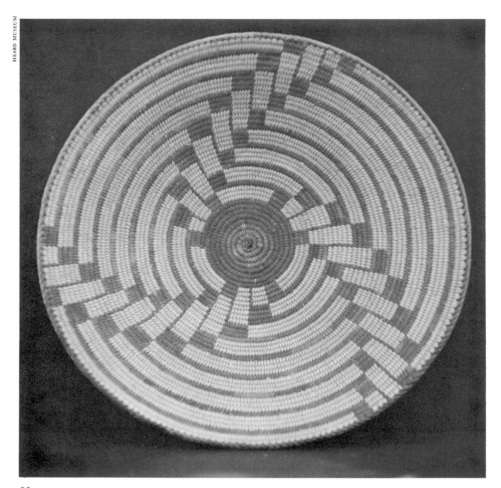

Hwa

Weaving a basket. This is sacred. My husband told me. His grandmother was one of those, a medicine woman. You should teach only your own family but if someone else comes to learn, she has to say the right words. Then she can learn. This happened to his grandmother. Someone from outside the family asked to learn to weave. She asked the right way and she taught her.

PIMA BASKET WEAVER

HABITAT

THE PIMA INDIANS live on two reservations in southern Arizona: the Gila River Reservation is located south of Phoenix on the Gila River; and the Salt River Reservation lies just east of Scottsdale, near the confluence of the Verde and Salt Rivers.

The region is low desert with several high mountain ranges to break the monotony of the plain. Most of the year the weather is intensely hot and dry, relieved only by short rainy seasons and a balmy winter.

The Pima adapted their needs and arts to this harsh environment. The cacti and wild plants supply a variety of foods which were generally cooked rather than eaten raw. Unlike the wide variety of plant life found in Pomo and Yurok territory in California, the materials used by the Pima are limited to the willow and cattail bordering the rivers, and the devil's claw of the open desert.

HISTORY

THERE IS SOME controversy whether the Pima are the direct descendants of the Hohokam who occupied the region from 300 B.C. to 1400 A.D. The first Spanish contact was in 1694, when Father Eusebio Francisco Kino made the first of six expeditions from the south into Pimeria. He found a peaceful, farming people. The Spaniards called them *Pima,* which means "I don't know," the answer given by a Pima to the question, "What is your name?"

The Pima call themselves *O'odham* or People, and to distinguish themselves from their closely related neighbors of a more arid environment, the Papago, they use the term *O'odham Akimole,* or River People.

The Pima have lost many of their old ways, but several of the women continue to make baskets. In so doing they hope to continue their culture and provide an added income for the family. And the weaving is sheer pleasure for them.

No longer does the young girl make her first basket upon her first menstruation. Once she would have

51

made one or more baskets for her puberty ceremony, and presented them to the older woman who was caring for her. Today the girl of about ten years most likely learns basket weaving in the classroom. But this craft is still a process of the mind in relation to one's culture and environment. It is a reminder of continuity, of seasons coming and going, of designs that are handed down from teacher to student without name.

USES

THE TRADITIONAL SHAPE for a Pima basket was a fairly shallow bowl with slightly rounded bottom and flaring sides, approximately fifteen inches in diameter and five inches in height. This was ideal for the important task of winnowing and parching wheat. The size of the basket varied considerably for use in other household chores, such as collecting and preparing squash, pumpkins, roots, beans, wild spinach, and fruits of the various cacti. A special very deep large basket was used to hold *tiswin,*

a liquor made from the saguaro fruit. This was gathered in June, the harvest marking the beginning of the Pima year.

As an old Pima woman told me, "They used to line the basket with mesquite pitch so they could put liquid in it. They would put the stew in a large basket, and everyone would dip in with their hands, even the children. People put back in the bowl what they couldn't eat. They'd take the bones and dry them up on the roof and use them again. They still had their flavor. They weren't afraid of flies in those days."

Baskets were also carried on the head in the Basket Dance. These were not used for food.

The utilitarian baskets have long ago been abandoned for the more easily obtained metal kitchen wares, although the traditional shapes are still woven for the tourist or collector. Other forms, such as plaques, shallow or deep bowls with straight sides, narrow-necked *ollas* and miniature baskets are examples of experimentation by the weavers.

MATERIALS

COMMON NAME	SCIENTIFIC NAME	PIMA	USE
Willow	*Salix nigra*	*ci'ol*	weft
Devil's claw	*Martynia frangrans*	*'ihuk*	weft
Cattail	*Typha augustifolia*	*'utwak*	warp

Gathering: Time and Place

The plants used in Pima basketry grow near water, except for the martynia. This is a weed, and used to grow readily in the deserts and fields before the white man plowed it under when preparing the ground for crops. It is still found in secluded low and high desert areas which have some moisture.

The women on the Salt River Reservation who weave baskets grow their own materials beside their homes. You can do the same quite easily; the willow branches may be selected carefully from a young tree only eight feet high.

The WILLOW is picked in the spring, during March and April. The new branches have begun to turn from bright green to light brown, and the secondary growth that will cause notches to show up on the prepared material has not yet appeared. There is also a second willow harvest in Arizona, the end of the summer between the last of July and the beginning of September. Much of the growth pattern depends on rainfall, so the tree should be checked during these periods once a week or so to determine the ripeness. Do not feel anxious that the picking season will only last a short time, as some branches on one tree may be ready earlier than others.

The CATTAIL is collected in late summer, about July or August, when it is green and the head is still quite firm. You will have to wade into fairly deep water, which has proved disagreeable for me at times, as what seemed like a clear pond turned out to be a stinking, black mudhole. The men often help the women with this task.

The MARTYNIA is taken in the autumn, about November. The soft green shield has just begun to peel away, revealing the hard, black claws. Some women disagree on this — I once picked the *'ihuk* before the green pod had broken open, and the claws became moldy. Therefore, I would suggest waiting a bit later till almost all the claw shows, but be careful that it is not exposed to the sunlight for long as it bleaches. Look in open sunny places; this plant needs little water, which may account for the fact that the Papago weavers, who live near Tucson and have a more arid land than the Pima, use more martynia in their baskets. The black or white seeds in the pod at the base of the hook can be eaten raw, or planted for future growth.

Method of Gathering and Preparing Materials

WILLOW

1. Cut the younger branches at the base near the larger branch, stack and take all together to a cool place to prepare further.

2. With your hands, strip the green leaves off in one motion.

3. Take a sharp knife and make a small lengthwise incision at the butt end of the branch.

4. Now you are ready to use your teeth! This initial splitting took me six hours to learn, but once it is mastered the technique will apply to the finer splitting later on. So . . . take one side of the split between your front teeth, the other side in your left hand, and using your right hand as a guide for pressure, with the thumb behind the split side which is held in your mouth, pull gently down and out with your left hand. Now you have two equal halves. It's all a matter of evenness, as the branch will naturally split in equal sections. This technique is fully illustrated in the Pomo chapter where Mollie Jackson prepares root the same way.

5. Take one section and slip your right forefinger under the bark at the butt end, steadying the willow with your thumb and left hand, and strip off the bark in one motion. This depends on the exact ripeness, and sometimes I have to scratch a bit at it. Never mind, it should all come off more or less easily.

6. You now have a pile of fresh-smelling, white, split, debarked willow. Take a bunch you can hold comfortably in your hand, even up the butt end, or end of the branch, and twist this into a very tight circle, the tips being on the outside. This will resemble a lariat loop. Use the pile of leftover bark strippings for string to tie this together. Storage method is the same here as illustrated for Pomo materials.

These coils of willow can be kept in a shaded place for years. An air-tight can is ideal as it will also exclude any dampness.

CATTAIL

1. Cut the stem of the cattail at the water line with a very sharp knife, gather as many as you can hold, and wade out of the bog.

2. Cut off the top.

3. Split the stalks in two down the center by drawing your knife down the length of the stalk.

4. Lay them in the sun to dry. The

stalks will bleach to off-white in color, and curl inwards.

5. Tie a bunch together and store in a shaded place for future use.

MARTYNIA

When the soft green outer covering falls off, there are two hard inner hooks connected to the seed pod. These hooks are black in color, and are the material used in weaving the design elements of the basket. The martynia can be stored as is, hooking a few together and then continuing to hook the rest on top.

These bunches can be as large as two feet in diameter, and will keep indefinitely in a dry, dark place. Further preparation is usually postponed until just before weaving.

MAKING THE BASKET

Tools

AWL. The Pima awl was formerly made from a cactus thorn, bone or piece of mesquite wood. The thorn may have been set in a gum handle made from the secretion of a tiny desert insect. Today awls are bought, or made from needles set in wood: willow, cottonwood or mesquite.

KNIFE. A large kitchen knife is necessary for cutting the coarse materials, but for the splitting and final scraping of the willow, martynia and cattail, a small knife is used, preferably a good penknife.

Hooking martynia pods together

Basketry materials, l. to r.:
pounding stone
basket starts
prepared willow tied in bundles
unsplit martynia pods
cattail for warp
awl
knife
prepared willow weft soaking

Splitting willow strand for weft

TIN LID. The tin lid of, say, a jar of instant coffee is needed for sizing the willow and martynia. Holes of varying sizes are punched in this with your awl.

BOWL. A bowl approximately ten inches in diameter is needed for soaking the materials.

Method

WILLOW

1. Soak the split willow in warm water for about fifteen minutes. If soaking is prolonged, the material will turn brown.

2. Take your small penknife and duplicate the initial splitting process, this time being very careful, as the material is more likely to break.

3. Insert the willow strip in the sharp side of one hole in the tin lid sizer, and pull it through. This strips off the edges and ensures an even width. Experiment on the size of the hole. It depends on how wide you want the materials to be, and this depends on the size of your basket — smaller strips for a smaller basket, generally.

4. Shape a small point in the smaller end of the willow to be used as the "needle end" in coiling.

CATTAIL

The final splitting for this material is simply done by continuing to split the stalk in half and half again till good narrow wands are produced.

Usually about three or four splits

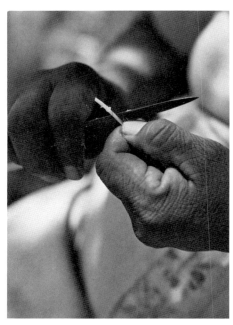

Cutting sharp point at tip end of willow weft

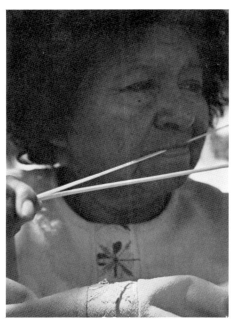

Splitting cattail for warp

will do this. Throw away the pithy inner core.

MARTYNIA

1. Prolonged soaking (two hours in hot water) is necessary as this material is the hardest in the basket, and is therefore employed in the areas that get maximum wear: the bottom and rim. Or if you prefer the old way of softening, bury it overnight in wet sand.

2. The whole pod is then split in two, and a single claw placed on a piece of wood.

3. Take your awl, and make a hole as close to the sharp end as possible, drawing the awl to the end so that there is a small slit.

4. Put one section between your front teeth, and split off the other half. This is done in the same way as splitting the willow. You will only be able to split as far down as the seed pod. Cut this off, and keep the seeds for planting.

5. Take one half at a time and repeat the process in order to separate the black outer covering from the white pithy core, which is discarded.

6. To achieve an even width, pull the martynia through the tin lid sizer.

Beginning the Basket

The beginning is known as *ache-dah,* and is the most difficult part of the basket.

There are three ways to start: a knot, a wrapped start, and a plaited start. This last one is seen in old baskets, but, to my knowledge, is not used any more.

The knot is a square knot or "just any knot." For this use four, five, or six pieces of martynia, and an extra

Making slit in martynia to begin the splitting

Splitting martynia

one for the sewing. The cattail is added right away if it is to be a large basket, but if not, the initial martynia is used up before the cattail is added as foundation.

The wrapped start is the most common.

1. Take several pieces of wet, prepared cattail, and tap the ends to even them up.

2. Holding this bundle, with the evened ends to the right, take a wet prepared piece of martynia or willow.

3. Begin wrapping this martynia or willow piece around the cattail sticks, starting at the *right hand end* of the cattail bundle.

4. Secure the martynia or willow well as you wrap it towards the middle of the bundle.

5. Do this for about one-quarter inch.

Starting the basket: wrapping willow weft strand around cattail

Wrapping willow

Wrapping willow

The start is folded back

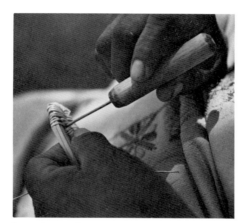

Inserting awl

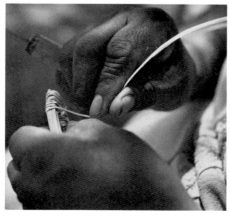

Coiling with willow

6. Fold this one-quarter inch back against itself into a closed "U" shape.

7. Insert the awl into the cattail sticks that are doubled back, thus making a hole. Withdraw the awl, and stick the martynia or willow strip left from the cattail wrapping process through this hole. Make the first holes rather close together.

All this time keep the materials wet.

8. As you proceed, the awl should be stuck between each stitch of martynia or willow on the previous row, sometimes putting two stitches in one hole, or splitting the martynia stitch of the prevous row, as the circle is expanding quite rapidly at this point.

9. To keep the coils flat, pound your basket start against a flat surface.

Adding New Materials

1. To add a new piece of martynia or willow, simply leave the old end sticking out the back of the basket to be cut off later. (Back of basket is the outside of the bottom. Conversely the front of the basket is the surface you are always looking at while working.) The weaving is tight enough so that this does not slip through. Add a new piece in a new hole, pulling it through so just the butt end is showing, put it over the cattail bundle and through the same hole again, thereby securing the end. Continue to work this piece till it is too short.

2. Cattail is added continually as the basket progresses in size. The

width of the bundle should increase gradually and remain constant from about the fourth row onwards. When a cattail stick is almost used up, push a new stick into the center of the bundle, and continue coiling. You will notice that the sticks will be at odd lengths so that adding will be staggered.

If using martynia, work till the size of the bottom is in proportion to what you have planned for the finished basket.

3. The last martynia stitch must be opposite the first one. For a good beginning basket of ten inches, the center is approximately three inches. You should follow your own preference. The examples in this book are traditional Pima designs, showing a variety of uses of the dark martynia against the light willow. This is often dependent on the amount of martynia available at the time.

4. When the bottom area is completed, the design is begun with the prepared willow, or in the case of a willow start, black stitches are now added.

Form

Form of the basket is dependent on the angle at which the awl is placed in the foundation. If the awl is pushed perfectly horizontally through the cattail, and withdrawn at the same angle, and the bundle kept directly on top of the previous row, the basket

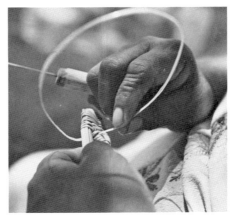

Coiling

Pounding basket start

Beginning the design

will progress with a flat form. This is the technique used to shape the martynia bottom. But if the awl is pushed horizontally through the bundle, and withdrawn at a slight angle downwards, and the bundle pulled slightly towards you, the basket will describe a soft curve inwards. This is the common *hwa* form. Care should be taken not to let the curve form too quickly.

By now you should be working with the design, using both willow and martynia. Note in the illustrations under the Design section that the martynia stitches are added to the left of the preceding stitch in the lower row. This is to ensure a straight line.

Finishing Off

When the design is completed, several plain willow rows may be made and the basket finished off. The last row should taper slowly, using less and less cattail in the bundle till the row ends directly opposite the last martynia stitch in the bottom area.

Martynia is always used for finishing off, which may be done in either of two ways: the simple overlay stitch or the false braid. For the overlay stitch, insert two pieces of martynia in the last willow row, two stitches apart. Then insert each piece four stitches to the left of its previous position. As an alternative, you may start the two pieces one stitch apart and progress at two-stitch intervals.

In the false braid method, only one piece of martynia is used, where two are used simultaneously in the overlay method. To make the false braid, insert the martynia between two willow stitches near the upper edge of the last row. Go over the top and count off six willow stitches to the left. Insert the martynia, bring it over the top again, and count off four willow stitches to the right.

Cut off all the loose ends of willow and martynia, rub the basket over with a smooth stone, wash lightly, and your "Pima" basket is done.

DESIGN OF THE BASKET

PIMA BASKET DESIGNS are predominantly geometric, the most common motifs being the fret, the whorl and the equal-armed cross. At the beginning of this century, some animal forms were introduced, such as the horse, deer, horned toad and gila monster. Human figures also gained some popularity, either full figures or two rows of half figures, interspersed with other elements.

The basket design is read as a black pattern on a white background. Martynia is used for the black, and willow for the white. After the bottom is completed, the weaver starts her design with a series of black "arms." There may be three, four, five, six or seven starts, but three, four or five are the most common. The pattern radiates from the center, other elements being added to fill in the blank spaces which occur as the basket expands.

It is often advised to use the single fret for your first basket. This is an old design "used in weaving cotton belts," according to a Pima weaver. More ambitious designs may be attempted later, culminating in the most complex, the squash blossom. Although it has been found that this is a more recent design, the Pima favor it, and admire the skill involved in its weaving. The followng designs have been illustrated in great detail so that you may follow the pattern closely in weaving your own basket.

1. Fret
2. Whirlwind
3. Turtleback
4. Three-armed cross
5. Elder Brother's House (*Se-'e-he Ki*)
6. Squash blossom

Unfinished basket: turtleback *design*

Turtleback *design*

Detail of turtleback *design*

Squashblossom design

The Pima woman keeps the entire design in her head as she weaves, never having to put it on paper. But she does count stitches as she goes along so that the pattern is balanced and the lines are either straight or perfectly curved. Geometric precision is a requirement for a good basket. Although the designs are traditional, each woman is expected to vary them according to her own individual creativity. I have never seen two Pima baskets alike.

Pima basket design still pervades the culture. The Gila River Reservations uses the squash blossom for its tribal seal, and the Salt River community uses the *Se-'e-he Ki*. This design tells the story of *Se-'e-he* or Elder Brother, who built his house as a maze to trick the enemy when they came. The Pima women delight in telling this story while they handle the basket, and with their finger, follow the pathway into the heart of *Se-'e-he's* house.

Three-armed cross design

Detail of three-armed cross design, Da'as da

Elder Brother's House design, Se 'e he

4: The Navajo Basket

Ts'aa

She is weaving herself into the world ...

NAVAJO WEAVER

HABITAT

THE NAVAJO PEOPLE live on eigh-
teen million acres of land in northern
Arizona and New Mexico and southern Utah. This includes both reservation and non-reservation areas used
by the People. Within this area there
are valleys, upland plains, tablelands
and mountains. Elevations range
from thirty-five hundred to ten thousand feet. Much of the land is semi-
arid: there are red sandstone rocks in
fantastic shapes, gray sagebrush,
piñon and juniper, grasses, cacti, and
the blue sky, cloudless and brilliant.
Roads are made with regard to the
terrain: winding and bumpy, and im-
passable in deep snow or sand. Everything is accessible to the eye, and distance is measured by the desire to go
someplace, not by time or conve-
nience. It is a good place to live. The
People say:

I walk in front of me beautiful, I
walk behind me beautiful, under
me beautiful, on top of me beautiful, around me beautiful, my words
will be beautiful

I will be everlasting one, everything
will be beautiful!*

It is beautiful indeed, but looking
carefully one sees that the red earth is
in fact sand, and that a living must be
wrested from the land that is so be-
loved. The Navajo are not farmers
like the Pima of the low desert, with
their substantial rivers and their irri-
gation techniques. In this high land
streams are rare and rainfall unpre-
dictable. The People are essentially
sheepherders, with some income from
cattle and goats. There are subsistence
crops such as corn, beans, melons,
peaches and apricots.

The winters are cold and heavy
snows common from December to
May, while in the summers this open
land is exposed to constant heat. Families may therefore move their homes
in accordance with the seasons. Range
land around Tuba City, on the west-

*Leland C. Wyman, ed., *Beautyway: A
Navaho Ceremonial* (New York:
Pantheon, 1957), p. 141.

69

ern edge of the reservation, gives a good base for the winter camp, centered around the sheep, goats and cattle. The land cannot support the number of livestock it once did due to overgrazing, but animals can still find enough small plants and grasses. And there are numerous wells and ground seepage, enough for a family's needs. May is the time to think of moving to the summer camp. Crops are planted then, and several preliminary weekend trips may be made to pre-

pare for the eventual move. Livestock are driven across the plateau. The family settles into its summer place beside a running stream, pond, corn fields, apricot trees and melon patch. A large brush shelter is set up, as most activities will now take place outdoors. Quilts and brightly colored cloths are strung between cottonwood trees. The women sit in the shade of these canopies and, with newly cut branches, continue to weave their baskets.

Three Paiute weavers — mother and two daughters

HISTORY

THE NAVAJO AND APACHE are an Athabascan speaking group of people who, it is believed, came down from the north about 1100 A.D. Ancestors of the Apache moved on south, east and west into Arizona and New Mexico, while the ancient Navajo settled in the northwest corner of New Mexico. They expanded westward and south from this original ground, and now, numbering one hundred thirty thousand people, constitute the largest Indian tribe in the United States.

The Navajo or *Diné* (People) are vigorous, proud and resilient. They have suffered incredible hardships from the hostile policies of the U.S. Government, the most memorable being the Long Walk of 1864, when they were rounded up from remote canyons and mesas and literally driven to what was to be a new home — the barren Bosque Redondo of eastern New Mexico. In 1868 they returned.

Some of the People managed to elude the government soldiers during the roundup prior to the Long Walk. Among these were Navajos who took shelter with Paiute families at Navajo Mountain. It was at this time that my basket teacher, a Paiute, said her great-grandmother learned to weave the basket from the Navajo women.

Paiute women, mainly on the west-ern edge of the reservation, which still includes families at Navajo Mountain, continue to supply the basket for Navajo use. This, of course, was not always the case, as the fine old baskets were woven by Navajo women, but as the People came more in contact with the white man's objects, they adopted these metal or plastic vessels into the Navajo household. The basket became solely a ceremonial article, and taboos were established that made weaving more and more complex. As a result the craft was practiced by fewer women, and the Paiute weavers found a ready market for their own work. A Paiute family today may consist of three generations of weavers making baskets all year round, and always able to sell to the trading posts, where they are bought by either Navajos or tourists.

The Paiute living side by side with the People, and intermarrying with them, continue to speak their own language. They feel an estrangement, although from outward appearances of dress, architecture and economy there is no difference. But they remain on the outskirts of Navajo life, and even after weaving baskets for many years many have never seen them used in ceremonies. They are a minority, apparently in a secondary position.

On the other hand, the *Diné* flourish under their fierce nationalism. Sheer numbers and amazing stubbornness of purpose have contributed to keeping the People balanced between the old and the new. They are practical, yet eloquent. The Navajo Community College was established at Many Farms in 1968. A crafts program was set up to teach rug weaving, silversmithing, pottery, leather working, sash belt making, and basket making. Within the first three years, sixty women learned to make baskets in an area where, previous to this, only three women knew how to weave. The Arts and Crafts Board regulates the sale of crafts at several locations on the reservation. Baskets are sold as a craft item, but at the same time, back behind a butte or down a fifty-mile stretch of dirt road, they are still used in social and religious functions.

USES

THERE ARE TWO main types of Navajo basket: the bowl and the water jug. The bowl, simply known as *ts'aa* (basket), varies in size in both diameter and depth, but a standard measurement for an old basket might be ten by three and one-half inches. Older specimens, attributed to Navajo weavers, are deeper and seemingly more practical than the new shallow baskets Paiute women weave today.

The *Diné* still marry in the traditional way, and hold a "sing" or *hatal* for the curing of disease. At these events the basket is a ritual object and restrictions surrounding its use are adhered to. In the Navajo wedding ceremony, the man and woman meet at sundown in a specially prepared shelter. The basket is placed in front of them, filled with blue corn meal. They eat this, taking alternate bites, beginning at the east edge and moving clockwise. The guests then dip their fingers into the remaining meal and say a prayer. The basket is taken away by the groom's mother, and not seen during the rest of the night. She just puts it away — never uses it again. But "anyone can ask to borrow it for a *kinaaldá* (girl's puberty rite) and then return it."*

At a *hatal,* the basket may be used to hold yucca soap for hair washing, or as a receptacle for prayer sticks. Then after the prayers and songs are finished, it can be turned over and used as a drum all night.

As a food container, the basket held "corn bread and mush of wild seeds."† It was used for winnowing and parching seeds, in the manner of the other tribes described. These things are no longer done. Baskets were functioning in everyday life after the return from Bosque Redondo in 1868, but by 1938 were only seen in

*Navajo hand-trembler.

†C. Kluchhohn et al., *Navaho Material Culture* (Cambridge, Mass.: Harvard Univ. Press, 1971), p. 134.

ceremonies. The water jug also became obsolete, and was replaced by metal buckets.* It is still made upon request and can be large enough to hold two gallons. Coiled like the *ts'aa,* the jug is then covered with goat dung and coated inside and out with piñon pitch.

The weavers being taught at Navajo Community College are guarding their baskets for use within the Navajo community. Paiute weavers work to sell. Sings are held all over the reservation, and be it Navajo or Paiute made, the basket is used in all ceremonies, as it was in the old days.

*Harry Tschopik, Jr., "Taboo as a Possible Factor Involved in the Obsolescence of Navaho Pottery and Basketry," *American Anthropologist* 40(1938):257.

MATERIALS

COMMON NAME	SCIENTIFIC NAME	NAVAJO	PAIUTE	USE
Sumac	*Rhus trilobata*	*k'įį́*	*shuv*	warp, weft
Mountain mahogany (root)	*Cercocarpus betulifolius*	*tse'esdazh*	*donaam*	dye (weft)

Gathering: Time and Place

The SUMAC is collected when there are no leaves on the branches: in early spring or during October and November. Weavers from Navajo Mountain must travel to the other side of Paiute Canyon or go as far as Farmington, New Mexico or Blanding, Utah, where they buy it from the Ute people or cut it themselves. Paiute weavers I know near Tuba City also must travel for their sumac, but the Utes in Blanding are their "cousins," and one of them may come over to Tuba City with a bundle of unpeeled sticks and ask one of the women to make a basket. Other weavers mention Flagstaff, Arizona and Cortez, Colorado.

It is obvious Navajo and Paiute weavers expect to make a good day's trip to collect their materials, unlike the Pima, Pomo and Yurok, who have theirs within an hour's ride, even if it involves trade and arduous climbing and wading.

The MOUNTAIN MAHOGANY ROOT is found in high rocky places. It grows big near water. It should be dug out in the winter (although some contradictory information cites June as the best time for harvest).

*Method of Gathering
and Preparing Materials*

SUMAC

1. Cut the leafless branches. Store some as is for warp.

2. To prepare weft, cut butt end of branch into three sections about an inch deep.

3. Holding tip end of branch steady between your knees, take one section of butt end between teeth and other two sections in either hand, and gently pull downwards. Run your hands down the sumac as it splits, to keep it even and prevent one side from splitting off short.

4. Split again as described for willow in the Pima chapter.

Splitting sumac branch into three sections

Materials: sumac branches kept with bark on; split sumac, white and dyed

5. Dry in the sun for about three days.

6. To remove bark, hold butt end of branch in left hand with bark side held away from body.

7. Using a cloth to protect your right hand, slide it downward over the branch and the bark will come away.

8. Dry white sewing splints in the sun and tie in bundles for storage.

If sumac is stored without being split, it must be soaked for two days to a week before the weft splints can be prepared.

Sumac tied in cloth and hung out of the sun

MOUNTAIN MAHOGANY ROOTS

1. Pound the reddish outer bark, add to water, and boil for three hours.

2. Burn cedar or juniper needles to ash.

3. Mix these ashes with water and rub over the prepared sumac.

4. Add sumac to mountain mahogany bark decoction, and boil till the right color — a reddish brown — is obtained. (One weaver, Mrs. Kee Black, said she added a spot of commercial dye.)

For the black color, another weaver, Rose Ann Laughter, says, boil the prepared sumac in a solution of "water, charcoal and juniper sap."

Split sumac is tied in bundles and stored

TRADING POST DYES

In recent years, weavers have been relying more and more on commercial dyes. The colors thus produced are still pleasing, if a bit bright and

Knife used in Navajo/Paiute basketry. Note the split sumac weft soaking in bucket.

Testing the wet sumac weft for pliability. Note the sharpened ends.

lacking the subtle lustre of the plant dyes. Dye colors vary from brilliant red to orange-brown, all shades being acceptable. I recommend using them.

For the *red*: use two spoonfuls each of black, red, brown and yellow in water.

For the *black*: use any black dye in solution as directed.

Add the sumac to either solution, boil fifteen minutes. Take out and dry. Return to pan and boil another fifteen minutes.

MAKING THE BASKET

Tools

AWL. Gradations in size among the three tribal basketry styles can be rated as follows: the widest sewing splint is Navajo-Paiute, Pima is medium, and the Pomo is the narrowest. This is only a guide, based on observation, but I have used the same awl for all types.

KNIFE. The Navajo-Paiute knife is a large dull one. Any size will really do.

BOWL. Three bowls are necessary as the white, black and red sumac must be soaked separately.

Method

All materials must be soaked in warm water for about fifteen minutes before coiling begins.

This is the easiest basket to make as there is only one material involved, and coiling goes very fast: the sumac is longer and wider than the willow and roots in the other baskets. You can make a basket eight and one-half inches in diameter in three days, not including dyeing.

Soak the unsplit sumac branches you will use for the warp for at least two days before commencing work.

Prepared sumac need only be scraped over to eliminate the thick parts, and the tip end sharpened.

Beginning the Basket

1. Take a sumac branch, unsplit and unpeeled. Cut the butt end into four sections to a depth of about two inches.

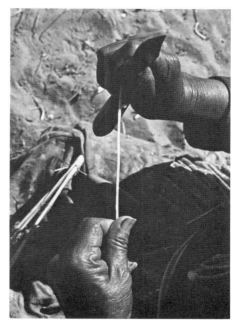

Scraping sumac

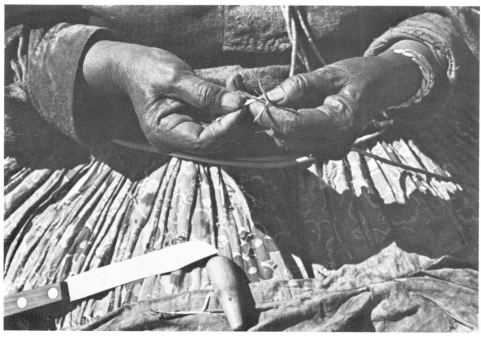

Starting the basket. Splitting the sumac branch into four.

2. Use your teeth, if possible, to remove the woody core from the length of each section.

3. Roll the four cut ends into as tight a circle as possible (the sumac branch will be sticking out to your left).

4. Take a piece of prepared white sumac, push the sharpened sewing end through the center hole, loop around the back, and back into the center hole. Continue to do this, working left to right or clockwise, till the full circle has been covered over. Each stitch should be right next to the previous one.

5. Reverse this wrapping. Work counterclockwise, and wrap over the foundation stick. (Hold work tightly and do not put it down at this point.)

6. Wrap another full round, being careful to space stitches evenly. The center hole should now be filled in.

7. Sharpen a new foundation stick. Cut the bark off the butt end for about four inches, and sharpen end. Rub a cloth over the entire stick to remove any rough buds. Insert new rod next to single warp rod, and continue coiling. (Note that you will be weaving over rods with the bark still on.)

8. With your awl, pierce, at about the halfway mark, the foundation rod of the previous row. Draw the sumac through this hole.

9. Continue to make holes with your awl, pulling the sumac through each hole made to the left of the stitch in the previous row. (The coiling technique has also been explained and illustrated in the Pomo and Pima chapters.) Go around three times — you will now be opposite the "start" or first stitch.

Looping sumac weft strand through center hole

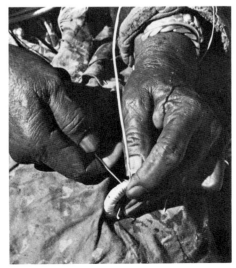

Making hole with awl. Note that the basket now has several sumac rods as warp.

Inserting sumac in hole made by awl

Close-up of awl in process. Note exactly where the awl hole is made in previous row, and position of the three warp rods.

Two starts and a partially completed basket. A full day's work by an experienced weaver.

Adding New Materials

1. To add new weft, take a prepared piece of sumac. Put through hole that the last stitch occupies. Pull through till end is flush with work surface. Make a new hole on left, push sumac through this, and pull tight at back of work. Continue coiling.

2. Gaps will appear between stitches, especially at the beginning of the basket. To fill them in, add two stitches where you would normally only put one, by splitting the stitch of the previous row in two.

3. To add new warp, when a foundation rod becomes too narrow, break it off even with the last stitch. Scrape the new rod to remove bark, and insert directly into the center or side of the old rod.

4. As you go along, you may break off loose ends of weft at the back of the work by twisting them around the awl and jerking. The dry material breaks off easily.

5. Adding the black (*doshuv* — Paiute): At this point, add another foundation rod, placing it at the *back of the other two*.

Note: How many black "mountains" you put in your basket is a matter of personal choice and affects the

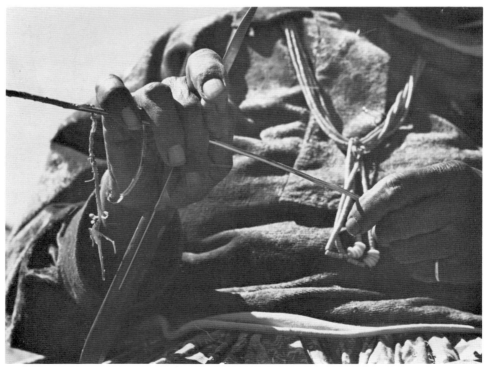

Scraping sumac before adding to basket start as new warp. Note position of the knife in hand.

final size of the basket. One basket with eight inner mountains measured fourteen inches in diameter. Fineness of stitch and depth of curve may determine the size. The pattern described in Steps 6–27 is that of my own first "Navajo" basket.

6. Put in three black stitches, just opposite the start.

7. Add the white (*tashuv*). Make eight stitches.

8. Continue pattern: three black, three white, etc.

9. Second row of pattern: make black twice as wide — they are stepping outwards. Nine black, six white, etc.

10. Third row of pattern: fifteen black, three white, etc.

11. Make three white stitches. This is the "pathway" (*pewaagh*).

12. Make three black stitches.

13. Add red (*kashuv*). Work all the way around.

14. Make three black stitches on top of last black stitches of previous row.

15. Make three white stitches for pathway.

16. Repeat for three red rows. (This may also vary. You may want to do only one or two. A large basket can take as many as five.)

17. Make the pathway. Add mountains in this row. As the basket is bigger, you will put in more mountains than before.

18. Make seven black stitches.

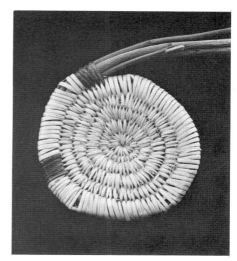

Adding the black or mountains

Adding the red. The inner black mountains are complete and one red row has been made, out of a possible two or three. Note the pathway woven in white, from the center out.

19. Make three white stitches.

20. Make approximately seven black stitches, lining the left side up with the left side of mountain in center of basket.

21. Repeat one round.

22. End last black stitch two stitches short of pathway.

23. Make eight white stitches.

24. Make five black stitches.

25. Repeat second row.

26. Make third row. Last three black stitches of mountain.

27. Make one plain row (*kashuv*).

Finishing Off

1. At starting point, insert weft and bring over to front of work.

2. Make hole with awl to the right and on top of last two stitches.

3. Pull weft through this hole.

4. Make one coiling stitch to left in previous row.

5. Bring forward and through top of work, two stitches to right, as before.

6. Repeat to make a figure eight or herringbone pattern all around the rim.

"In the ancient days a Navajo woman invented this pretty border. She was seated under a juniper tree, finishing her work in the old, plain way, when the god Hastseyath threw a small spray of juniper into her basket. Happy thought! She imitated the fold of the leaves on the border and the invention was complete."*

7. Begin tapering end about an inch from start. The basket should be finished off directly above the pathway. Cut one branch at a time.

The *Diné* believe this rim must be started and finished in one day — before sunset — or the weaver will go blind.

Form

All Navajo *ts'aa* are shaped like a shallow bowl. To form the curve of the basket, rest the warp rods *slightly* forward on the previous row. A rather bumpy surface is achieved, when using three-rod construction, by placing a larger warp rod in the front position. Number of warp rods may vary, although a Navajo weaver will use only odd numbers of warp rods in the foundation.

DESIGN OF THE BASKET

The center is the beginning of life, moving outwards. Then the rain comes. These are black clouds. The red lines are the red or pink in the sky and clouds. The outer white part is the increase of the People. This can be any size till the basket is finished. The pathway is to let the People emerge: a way out.

NAVAJO MEDICINE WOMAN

*Mason, p. 516.

THIS WEDDING BASKET design was used in the old days for all ceremonies, and still is. A medicine man will not take another basket. Designs in basket collections made before 1905 show at least seven other motifs, which may have been restricted to use in the home.

In every design, the *che'etiin,* or pathway, always appears. In the firelight at night, the medicine man can orient the *che'etiin* to the east by feeling the slope of the last stitches, which stop directly above the pathway.

The Navajo basket is sacred and filled with power. An old *ts'aa* has been, perhaps, in many sings, filled with corn meal and pollen, used for the ritual bath or as a drum. Do not play with it, and, if you weave the *ts'aa,* know that you may be creating a portion of your life.

Navajo wedding basket

Appendix

THROUGHOUT THIS BOOK I have spoken of the making of baskets from plants growing in particular areas familiar to four Indian peoples in the western United States. I realize that interested weavers may live in a more widespread area than that described. So for those to whom the traditional materials of this region are not available, I suggest some substitutes.

Indian women throughout the country used the locally indigenous plants. A number of Plains tribes made their coiled baskets from cottonwood branches, elm roots and yucca leaves. From the Great Lakes to the northeast coast, sweet grass (*Hierocloe odorata*) was used as the foundation and sewn with needle and thread. The Iroquois of New York State use corn husk which can be employed as both warp and weft in a basket. Farther south, in Louisiana, the Indian weavers used the leaf of the palmetto (*Inodes palmetto*) in a plain white coiled basket.

Willow has perhaps the widest distribution of any tree, and can be considered an important material in all geographic areas. Its advantage is that it can be used for both the warp, as in Pomo basketry, and the weft, as in the Pima basket. The simple difference is that the latter is split and the former is not. It can also be dyed with a commercial dye to produce a variety of colors for designs. Red ossier is a good Eastern equivalent to the sumac used by the Navajo. Cattail or tule is found in marshy areas along the Eastern seaboard. The criteria for choosing any plant material are strength and flexibility.

A more sensitive question is that of synthetic materials. My hands have no interest in them. But I do admire the skill and inventiveness of some extraordinary sculptural baskets that have been made in the last few years. They claim to be baskets, but are often not, if one defines a basket as an object which is made for use. Some of them cannot stand up: they crumble on one side in a limp weave, coil up eight feet tall like a sentinel, join together in large chimney pot groups, or are full of large holes. I do not know what an Indian weaver would say of these baskets: probably laugh, and say they weren't baskets, not baskets at all. A weaver must start somewhere, and like the young Indian girl who is given the materials for her first basket by her mother or grandmother, I say, begin where you sit. Look around, and use what's available. And if you can get out to Navajo or Yurok country, so much the better.

For the weaver who would like to experiment with form, texture and color, using traditional basketry techniques, I have listed some materials, both natural and synthetic, that are generally available in craft shops or in everyday life.

SUBSTITUTE MATERIALS FOR BASKETS

NATURAL	USE
Plant materials (see above)	weft, warp
Ropes and strings of various thicknesses	weft, warp
Raffia in different colors	weft
Horsehair	weft, warp
Wool	weft
Cane	warp
Straw	warp

SYNTHETIC	
Rags	weft
Magnetic tape	weft
Telephone wire	weft
Plastic bags	weft, warp
Garden hose	warp
Extruded tubing	warp
Shower curtain strips (plastic)	weft
Ribbon	weft

Glossary

BUTT END — The thickest end of a branch; end cut from larger branch.

COIL — Basketry technique in which a spiral foundation begins at the center and continues to the rim. Successive circles are sewn together with a pliable weft.

FOUNDATION — The core or inner bundle of coiled basketry, or the radiating stiff sticks of twined basketry.

HATAL — Navajo word for a curing ceremony.

MOUNTAINS — Descriptive word for the black terraced motifs in the Navajo basket.

PATHWAY — Narrow, light-colored band running from center to edge in the Navajo basket.

PLAIT — Basketry technique in which flat strips pass over and under each other, both being of equal size.

OVERLAY — In twined basketry, when an extra weft material is laid against and parallel with each of the structural wefts, producing a colored pattern on the outside, or inside, of the basket.

RANCHERIA — A Pomo village community made up of one or several settlements.

SPLINT — The pliable sewing material which coils around the bundle in coiled basketry.

START — The beginning stitches of any basket.

TANNIC ACID — An astringent substance in plants, such as the acorn, which is slightly poisonous.

TWINE — Basketry technique in which vertical foundation sticks are laid out like spokes of a wheel and bound at the crossing. These sticks are fastened by two or three weft strands which move in a continuous spiral from the central hub to the ends of the ribs, crossing each other between warps.

WARP — The foundation of a basket; in the coiled method the warp is made of multiple or bundle, rod or slat, and combinations of these; in the twined method the warp is the stiff radiating sticks around which the more flexible weft is run.

WEFT — The pliable sewing strand or strands in the basket; in the coiled method the weft is a single strand which wraps around the warp in successive coils; in the twined method the weft is worked in twos or threes, passing over and under the warp sticks in a variety of combinations.

Suggested Reading

AGINSKY, B. W. and E. G. *Deep Valley*. Stein & Day, N.Y. 1971

ALLEN, ELSIE. *Pomo Basketmaking*. Naturegraph Publishers, Healdsburg, Calif. 1972

BARRETT, S. A. *Pomo Indian Basketry*. University of California Publications, American Archaeology and Ethnology, vol. 8, 1908

BOAS, FRANZ. *Primitive Art*. Dover Publications, N.Y. 1955

BROWN, VINSON and ANDREWS, DOUGLAS. *The Pomo Indians of California and Their Neighbors*. Naturegraph Publishers, Healdsburg, Calif. 1969

DIXON, R. B. *Basketry Designs of the Indian of Northern California*. Bulletin, American Museum of Natural History, N.Y. XVII, 1902

EVANS, GLEN and CAMPBELL, T. N. *Indian Baskets*. Texas Memorial Museum, Austin, 1970

FEDER, NORMAN. *American Indian Art*. Harry Abrams, N.Y. 1971

FIELD, CLARK. *The Art and the Romance of Indian Basketry*. Philbrook Art Center, Tulsa, Okla. 1964

JAMES, GEORGE W. *Indian Basketry and How to Make Indian and Other Baskets*. The Rio Grande Press, N.Mex. 1903

KISSELL, MARY L. "Basketry of the Papago and Pima," Anthropological Papers of the American Museum of Natural History, vol. XVIII, part IV, N.Y. 1916

KLUCKHOHN, CLYDE and LEIGHTON, D. *The Navaho*. Doubleday & Co., N.Y. 1962

KLUCKHOHN, C., HILL, W. W. and KLUCKHOHN, L. C. *Navaho Material Culture*. Harvard University Press, Cambridge, Mass. 1971

KROEBER, A. L. *Basket Designs of the Indians of Northwestern California*. University of California Publications, American Archaeology and Ethnology, vol. 2, no. 4, 1905

———. "California Basketry and the Pomo," *American Anthropologist*, vol. XI, 1909

————. *Handbook of the Indians of California.* Bulletin 78 of the Bureau of American Ethnology, Washington, D.C. 1925

MASON, O. T. *Aboriginal American Basketry.* Annual Report of the Smithsonian Institution, 1902

MERRILL, RUTH E. *Plants Used in Basketry by the California Indians.* Acoma Books, Ramona, Calif. 1970

MILES, CHARLES and BOVIS, PIERRE. *American Indian and Eskimo Basketry.* Pierre Bovis, San Francisco, 1969

MORRIS, EARL H. and BURGH, ROBERT F. *Anasazi Basketry.* Carnegie Institution of Washington, Washington, D.C. 1941

Navajo School of Indian Basketry. *Indian Basket Weaving.* Whedon & Spreng Co., Los Angeles, 1903

O'NEALE, LILA. *Yurok-Karok Basket Weavers.* University of California Publications, American Archaeology and Ethnology, vol. 32, 1932

"Portrait of a Heritage," Valley National Bank, Phoenix, Ariz. 1971

ROESSEL, RUTH. *Navajo Studies at Navajo Community College.* Navajo Community College Press, Many Farms, Ariz. 1971

ROSEBERRY, VIOLA M. *Illustrated History of Indian Baskets and Plates.* Leo Brown, Orange Cove, Calif. 1915 (Reprinted 1973)

ROSSBACH, ED. *Baskets As Textile Art.* Van Nostrand Reinhold, N.Y. 1973

RUSSELL, FRANK. *The Pima Indians.* 26th Annual Report for 1904–05, Bureau of American Ethnology, 1908

SHAW, ANNA M. *Pima Indian Legends.* University of Arizona Press, Tucson, 1968

SIDES, DOROTHY S. *Decorative Art of the Southwestern Indian.* Dover Publications, N.Y. 1961

TSCHOPIK, HARRY, JR. "Taboo as a Possible Factor Involved in the Obsolesence of Navaho Pottery and Basketry," *American Anthropologist,* vol. XL, 1938

UNDERHILL, RUTH. "The Papago Indians of Arizona and their relative the Pima," U.S. Department of the Interior, 1941

WEBB, GEORGE. *A Pima Remembers.* University of Arizona Press, Tucson, 1959

WELTFISH, GENE. *Origins of Art.* Bobbs-Merrill, N.Y. 1953

WYMAN, LELAND C., ed. *Beautyway: A Navaho Ceremonial.* Text recorded and translated by Berard Haile and Maud Oakes, Pantheon, N.Y. 1957

About the Author

SANDRA CORRIE NEWMAN has affection and empathy for the American Indian, and is especially interested in the crafts created by him. She has spent more than seven years studying Indian crafts, language and traditions. Her professional experience and research have included affiliations with The Heye Foundation, The Heard Museum, The Museum of Navaho Ceremonial Art, Denver Art Museum, Rutgers University and The Lowie Museum of Anthropology. To this impressive list she has added field work on the Navajo, Salt River, Ukiah and Hoopa reservations and instruction in the languages of the Pima and Navajo.

Most importantly, her work has taken her into the homes of the families of people she writes about. They have shared with her not only their gathering and weaving techniques, but also their philosophy, their insights, their humor and their traditions. She has mastered the actual weaving processes and become aware of the rhythms of their lives and the significance of their crafts. All of these factors combine to make her thoroughly qualified to translate these skills and knowledge into this useful volume.